UNDER THE MERCY: CHARLES WILLIAMS AND THE HOLY GRAIL

by
Robert Peirano

the apocryphile press
BERKELEY, CA
www.apocryphile.org

apocryphile press
BERKELEY, CA

Apocryphile Press
1700 Shattuck Ave #81
Berkeley, CA 94709
www.apocryphile.org

Copyright © 2014 by Robert Peirano. All rights reserved. No part of this book may be used or reproduced in any manner whatsoever without written permission of the author. Printed in the United States of America.

ISBN 9781940671420

UNDER THE MERCY: CHARLES WILLIAMS AND THE HOLY GRAIL

by
Robert Peirano

Preface

Charles Walter Stansby Williams was a poet, novelist, playwright, theologian, biographer and historian whose position in British literary history is comparatively obscure. This volume intends to prove he does not deserve such obscurity.

Writers usually fall into one of two categories, major or minor. However, there are a few who fall into neither category. They are the writers whose imagination and vision soar beyond traditional parameters and patterns. Since their ability to shatter barriers of language and express ideas within new literary paradigms places them outside subjective or objective categorization, they are the exceptions to commonly encountered literary classifications. They dream the dreams and realize the realities that other writers can only aspire to. They are the true explorers of domains beyond conventional literature's expansive horizon. This is Charles Williams' intellectual and spiritual universe.

His novel, *War in Heaven*, and his Arthurian poems, *Taliessin through Logres* and *The Region of the Summer Stars*, exemplify his thinking, reposing far beyond the traditional literary horizon's observable limit. Williams' efforts represent a literary achievement measureable only in the qualitative terms of Transcendent Reality's imagery. Moreover, collectively, his endeavors illustrate his creative ability to metaphorically explore the cosmic movement of humankind from the Creation through the Fall. This metaphorical journey continues from the Fall through the experience of Incarnation and humanity's opportunity to, once again, dwell within God's grace through the Crucifixion and Resurrection.

The literary catalyst for this achievement is the Holy Grail. For Williams, the Grail Quest is a metaphor symbolizing humanity's effort to return to the Creator's benevolence. He believes the Grail is a dynamic medium, which absorbed the energy of the Last Supper, the Incarnation, the Crucifixion and the Resurrection. Thus, the miraculous Grail at the Mass' Eucharistic core is Transcendent Reality's continuous actualization throughout the ages, reflecting the co-inherent glory of the Father's truth, the Son's beauty, and the Spirit's wisdom.

Moreover, Williams gently guides us to a metaphysical understanding of the Holy Trinity, sharing a vision leading to an incomprehensible Entity in whose presence we find peace and comfort. As a result, we become Christ-conscious rather than self-conscious, inspired to live that new consciousness in everyday life.

Thus, Charles Williams is a conduit for us to an existence we knew before our conception and will know again upon our physical death. However, in the meantime, he makes us conscious that existence in the Holy Trinity is within reach, even in this our present state, through co-inherence. Williams is without question a major writer to those for whom Transcendent Reality's Divine Mercy is a core foundation of their faith.

Contents

Preface v

Chapter:

1. Introduction 1
2. War in Heaven 17
3. Charles Williams' Arthuriad 29
4. The Empire Ascendant: Revealing Possibilities 37
5. Auroral Logres: Possibilities of Brilliant Splendor 49
6. The Uncoupling of Empire: Seeds of Destruction 67
7. The Galahadian Ideal: Redemption Triumphant 85
8. Charles Williams' Literary Achievement 109
Acknowledgements 121
Works Cited 123
Works Consulted 127

They shall look and recognize themselves in Him, and Him in themselves, in their life, in their work, in the hidden knowledge of the Holy Grail, and in the service of the Holy Grail. And they shall worship Him, who will be inseparably with them.

Fr. Sergius Bulgakov
The Holy Grail and The Eucharist

They believe that the kingdom awaits them only in the afterlife, and so they miss the most important teaching: that we are to live on earth as it is in heaven, and create heaven where it does not exist on earth. The kingdom of God is for us, here and now, on earth and in our earthly bodies if we will only claim it. This is done through love and love alone… Pray in the manner I have shown you, at the center of the labyrinth and at the center of your life. Use the prayer as a rose and marvel at the beauty of its six petals for it contains all you need to find the kingdom of heaven on earth. The central circle is love perfected. The children of the world must open their eyes to see God all around them. Then they can live as love expressed. It is in doing this that they fulfill their destinies, and likewise their promises to and from eternity. They must awaken. And they must awaken now. Love Conquers All. For those with ears to hear, let them hear it.

Kathleen McGowan
The Book of Love

Chapter 1

Introduction

Charles Walter Stansby Williams (1886-1945) was a British author/poet who is almost unknown today in British literary history. In Great Britain, there is a small active Charles Williams Society dedicated to preserving his works. In the United States, his memory and work live on in the archives of the Marion E. Wade Center of Wheaton College, Wheaton, Illinois. Here a researcher can find an extensive collection of Williams' works, including a set of his personal journals. It seems only a small coterie of followers continues to admire and study his creative efforts in his homeland and in the United States. This work proposes that he deserves greater recognition in literary history.

Those who know Charles Williams probably do so because of his association with the famous British literary group, the Inklings, most of whom were faculty members at Oxford University. It was an informal group that gathered to discuss one another's works in progress. Here, for example, J.R.R. Tolkien first tested his ideas for *The Lord of the Rings* trilogy, and C. S. Lewis read aloud his *Chronicles of Narnia*. Listening intently might be Owen Barfield, lawyer and author; Warren Lewis, the brother of C. S. and a noted historian in his own right; Charles Williams, author and lecturer at Oxford University; and other Oxford locals such as Nevill Coghill and Adam Fox, the Dean of Divinity at Magdalen College.[1] As new members were invited to join the group, an observer might notice among the new arrivals Byzantine scholar and Catholic priest, Father Gervase Mathew. Alan Jacobs has asserted that

> there were limits to the Inklings' charity, both to one another and to outsiders, but consistently, they were indeed a fellowship of friends whose pleasure was simply in the company of one another and who had no mutual obligations, but in mutual love offered strength, encouragement and sympathy.[2]

If Charles Williams is remembered at all, he is perhaps best remembered for the dark characters and mystical circumstances that appear in his seven novels, with characters and plots revolving around magical powers capable of controlling the evil dimensions of the universe. Because of these vivid portrayals, many believed that Williams was a dabbler in the "dark arts." In fact, at a time when "spiritualism" was at its peak in post-World War I England, Charles Williams was associated with the Order of the Golden Dawn, a spiritualist group led by poet W. B. Yeats. He later disassociated himself from this group and became a member of the Fellowship of the Rosy Cross (FRC), which was headed by the spiritual mystic A. E. Waite and included members such as T. S. Eliot and Evelyn Underhill, author of the famous tome, *Mysticism*.

The FRC was attuned to humankind's spiritual relationship to the Divine, emphasizing mysticism as the medium for forming this connection. However, even here Williams did not find the answers to his lifelong spiritual questions. He, T. S. Eliot and Evelyn Underhill eventually resigned from the FRC and began their individual pursuits toward the special Divine coalescence they sought.

Williams' path emerged from his deeply held faith in the Church of England, enabling him to express his understanding and beliefs through his novels and plays. He also wrote extensively on history, biography and theology. His poetry, for which he wanted to be remembered most, was often seen as dense and obscure. Eliot once confided to C. S. Lewis that "he [Eliot] could never make heads or tails of it. Lewis, however, did understand the poetry of Williams fairly well, and developed a deep appreciation of it."[3]

Between 1912 and 1945, Charles Williams published at least seven volumes of poetry, concluding this aspect of his work with the classics *Taliessin through Logres* and *The Region of the Summer Stars*, two unique cycles within his planned larger Arthuriad. During the years 1929-1948, his seven full-length plays were produced, perhaps the most noteworthy of which is *Thomas Cranmer of Canterbury*. Williams' most popular and commercially successful works, his novels, were published between 1930 and 1948. These consistently pitted the dark forces of evil against the Christian forces of good. The most famous is *All Hallows Eve*, published posthumously in 1948 and containing a poignant introduction by his friend T. S. Eliot.

In addition, from 1919 to 1943, Williams published seven major theological works, the most well known being *The Descent of the Dove* (1939), which, as W. H. Auden argued, represents the key to understanding Williams and his overall vision. The other work equally appreciated for its insight is *The Figure of Beatrice* (1943), one of the numerous critical works Williams produced between 1930-1945.

Cumulatively, Charles Williams' publications, including his editorial works and prose that appeared in respected journals such as the *Dublin Review*, *Time and Tide*, the *New English Weekly*, and the *London Mercury*, total in the hundreds, even without his reviews of detective stories for the *Sunday Times* and other notable British newspapers.

A prolific writer, a significant writer, a relevant writer, Charles Williams was all of these and more. A remarkable literary artist, he still remains one brief memory from anonymity and obscurity. A demonstration of this possibility appears by his listing among the authors noted in *The Lost Club Journal*, the subtitle of which is *A Journal of Literary Archaeology*. Included among the Lost Club are: Edward Bulwer-Lytton, Ronald Fraser, Arthur Ransomme, Althea Gyles, H. Rider Haggard and Charles Williams.[4] Despite this "lost" company that Charles Williams is associated with, at least in the minds of some, one must agree with Bernadette Bosky that Charles Williams deserves better. Ms. Bosky states:

> Though Williams has never become as famous as Lewis and Tolkien, attention to his life and works has continued to grow in a kind of punctuated evolution. Williams has been written about by those who knew him—[including] Anne Ridler, correspondent Lang-Sims, coworker and biographer Alice Mary Hadfield, and more famous friends such as C. S. Lewis, T. S. Eliot and W. H. Auden—and by those attracted to his fiction, poetry, plays, theology, literary studies, historical writing, life and personality.
>
> Charles Williams remains a most unusual author whose work leaves few readers neutral. Though some find his writing

occasionally obscure, his novels appeal to many readers of fantasy and science fiction, offering a combination of myth with adventure, deep psychological insights with everyday life. [The] supernatural and mythic elements may attract such readers to Williams' poetry and plays as well. Finally, the unity of Williams' thought may [also] draw readers to the nonfiction, from reviews to theological studies and biographies, in which one can fully experience the integrity of Williams' art and ideas.[5]

I vividly remember my first encounter with the vision of Charles Williams as I read his novel *War in Heaven*. My initial impression was that it was a fairly good story, a little archaic in language because it had been published in 1930. However, as I became more involved, the story seemed to draw me into a vortex of descending concentric circles, much like Dante's *Inferno*. Each circle drew me closer and closer to the evil Joseph Conrad had explored in his novel, *Heart of Darkness*. At the core of the vortex, Williams confronted me with the evil that lay just beyond the horizon of the novel's words and the reader's mind, an intense evil lurking in the darkness. However, I could not see it until Williams was ready to expose it and, subsequently, lead me back to the light.

Then he drew me once again into his Dantean world, only now the concentric circles were ascending. Slowly, a healing process took place for the characters and for me. Implicitly, the co-inherent characters, those who did not live for themselves but rather for others, knew all along that they must and could survive their struggle against evil; their simple trust and faith would secure their emergence. I began to understand the journey of discovery Charles Williams had shared with me and sensed that his vision was unique, even though I did not then, nor do I now fully comprehend it. As a consequence, one goal of this study is to understand more, if not all he offers.

The heart of that understanding lies embedded in a scene described in chapter ten of *War in Heaven*. The three protectors of the Grail are: Kenneth Mornington, a publisher's clerk, who seeks to save the classical Grail of Malory and Tennyson; the Duke of North Ridings, a poet and devout Roman Catholic, who sees only the consecrated Grail of his Church, representing Christ's Last Supper; and the Archdeacon Julian Davenant, who sees in the Grail the sacred vessel of the Holy Eucharist. They also represent Williams' contemporary version of the Arthurian protectors of the Holy Grail:

Bors the everyman, Percivale the poet, and Galahad the purest knight. They realize that an evil telepathic attack has begun on the Grail. The Archdeacon commands: "Make yourselves paths for the Will of God... Pray, pray in the name of God. They are praying against Him tonight."[6]

At this point, Williams describes a clash of cosmic wills between the three "knights" and the forces of evil that are aligned against them in their efforts to protect the Holy Grail. It lies at the core of the matter with which the novel deals. The core's nucleus will witness the assumption of the natural mind into the supernatural. This is the co-inhering experience Williams offers his readers.

Moreover, this scene articulates the metaphysical vision of the author in unparalleled language. For example, when Mornington begins to feel the psychological pressure of the attack, Williams verbalizes Mornington's thought process as follows:

> It crossed Kenneth's mind, as he sank on his knees, that if God could not be insulted, neither could he be defied, nor in that case the progression and retrogression of the universe disturbed by the subject motion of its atoms. But he saw, running out like avenues, a thousand metaphysical questions, and they disappeared in the excitement of his spirit.[7]

Furthermore, when the Duke cries out, in a moment of despair, demanding to know, "against what shall we pray?" the Archdeacon responds "against nothing… Pray that He that made the universe may sustain the universe that in all things there may be delight in the justice of His will."[8] What begins to materialize from this response is a "common consciousness of effort." It is the interior energy of the priest that will consume the three with the reality that, in the face of this onslaught, active opposition is futile. Rather, they must transport the natural human response elicited from this struggle to a place of repose and active passivity in the mind of the Supernatural. To truly be in union with the Divine, silence must prevail, thus allowing the One to enter the blocked channels of Orthodoxy's intellect. Moreover, this commonality of participation by the three companions causes them to accomplish a co-inherence with each other, free of distraction and full of vivid apprehension.

In this moment of immovable calm, Williams describes the individual assaults on each. The Duke will be aware of the presence of evil through the sound of "soft footprints." For Mornington, there will be taunts of remembrance of past "casual contempts," the use of "idle words" and a "certain regretful attention to these." Mornington will respond by forgiving himself these missteps. If one is to be truly freed by the intensity of the sacrifice of the Word Incarnate, this is the greatest act of forgiveness an individual soul may exert.

Williams continues: "Yet the attack went on: to one a footstep, a whisper, a slight faint touch; to another a gentle laugh, a mockery, a reminder; to the third a spiritual pressure which not he but that which was he resisted."[9] Here, the author demonstrates a spiritual awareness, using his distinctive literary technique of obfuscating the universal unseen realities of time and space. The three are being overpowered by a malevolence that they, alone and individually, cannot resist. However, the incongruent image that Williams projects is of a Power much greater than the three, not only assisting them in this spiritual struggle between good and evil, but also becoming co-inherent with them. They and the Other have become one unity. The exchange is complete and, as a result, the evil cannot overwhelm the good in this titanic struggle. The Grail will be saved from destruction.

Williams goes on:

> The Graal vibrated still to the pressure, more strongly when it was accentuated, less and less as the stillness within and amidst the three was perfected. Dimly he [the Archdeacon] knew at what end the attack aimed; some disintegrating force was being loosed at the vessel—not conquest, but destruction was the purpose, and chaos the eventual hope. Dimly, he knew that, though the spirit of [the evil] Gregory formed the apex of that attack, the attack itself came from regions beyond Gregory. He saw, uncertainly but sufficiently defined, the radiations that encompassed the Graal and the fine arrows of energy that were expended against it. Unimportant as the vessel itself might be, it was yet an accidental storehouse of power that could be used, and to dissipate this material centre was the purpose of the war. But through the three concentrated souls flowed reserves of the power which the vessel retained; and gradually to the priest it seemed, as in so many celebrations, as if the Graal itself was the centre—yet, no longer the Graal, but a greater than the Graal.

Silence and knowledge were communicated to him as if from an invisible celebrant; he held the cup no longer as a priest, but as if he set his hands on that which was itself at once the Mystery and the Master of the Mystery. But this consciousness faded almost before it was realized; his supernatural mind returned into his natural, leaving only the uncertainty that for the time at least the attack was ended.

"It is done," he said. "Whatever it was has exhausted itself for the time. Let us go and rest."[10]

In *War in Heaven*, Charles Williams expresses a command of language that opens the dimensions of time and space in the universe to a degree I had never experienced before. Moreover, Williams' words describe dimensions beyond these two, dimensions of spirituality I knew existed, but of which I had little comprehension until I read his work. Five years later, my understanding is still incomplete. Who among us will ever fully understand Charles Williams' many dimensions?

My search, to answer why this is so, inspired a personal quest to visit the mind of Charles Williams. I had to try to find out how he had acquired a depth of understanding of the infinite and of spiritual ecstasy perhaps tasted only by the saints. I wondered, "How could a writer have the mind to understand, much less the ability to communicate an otherworldly vision in written form with such clarity, emotion and spirituality? How could a writer overcome the natural barriers of the written word so skillfully?" It was as though he had the capacity to see and explain in precise language what ordinary minds could never fully comprehend, and an equivalent distinct gift that empowered him to present a glimpse of the eternal.

Through his symbolic language, Charles Williams represented ideas and imaginative scenes in a way I had never previously encountered. He seemed to have a vivid personal knowledge of everything he was writing about: the good, the evil and the eternal. I realized that his was a mind worthy of close examination, and I sensed that no matter how vigorously I might try, I would never fully penetrate the depths of his covenant with the Infinite. However, I needed to try to understand what he was offering, because he touched me at a very personal level. Perhaps I was meant to meet him at this point in my life. I do not believe in coincidences.

I leave the reader to ponder these words of Charles Williams, which, I believe, express a significant portion of the spiritual paradigm he envisioned:

> "Death you shall have at least," [Prester John] said. "But God only gives, and He has only Himself to give, and He, even He, can give it only in those conditions which are Himself. Wait but a few years, and He shall give you the death you desire. But do not grudge too much if you find that death and heaven are one."[11]

Unless relevancy and significance are simply different dimensions of the same prism, it is perfectly fair and reasonable to ask about the relevancy of Charles Williams and his writing as distinct from its significance. Or is it simply a matter of splitting hairs to consider them unique in the focus they bring to a topic?

The Oxford English Dictionary (OED) defines "relevant" as "appropriate or applicable in the (esp. current) context or circumstances: having social, political, etc., relevance."[12] The subject in question must be applicable to some dimension of the current state of affairs. In contrast, the word "significance" implies a completely different focus. If a topic is significant, then it is meaningful and important in and of itself. Again, according to the *OED*, it is "full of meaning or import; a hypothetical quality, thought to be common to all great works of art, that evokes an aesthetic response and is considered to be more significant than the subject matter."[13] Something may be significant, but not relevant, or relevant and not significant, or both relevant and significant.

If we use Charles Williams to demonstrate this point, he and his works are extremely significant. He developed a distinct and important personal vision, the best example of which is his Arthurian cycle of poetry, expressed with eloquence if not always clarity. However, that significance does not necessarily suggest his work is in any way germane to the current state of affairs, either in the world in general, or in the reader's life in particular.

Also, he can be considered a relevant composer of both prose and poetry. His work had a very relevant impact upon my life. I read *War in Heaven*, and Williams' words stretched across seventy-six years of time, space and the universe to touch me as I had never been touched before. Aside from my personal experience, however, does he have relevance for the world? I propose to show that he does. In my opinion, his works are full of meaning and import, and they have the hypothetical quality that evokes an aesthetic response more significant than the subject matter.

Furthermore, if Williams is a major writer, he must speak to the current age through his work. The remainder of this section argues that Charles Williams is as relevant today as he was during the first half of the twentieth century, because he satisfies three criteria. First, he establishes the framework for a "good community" based upon the three root concepts, co-inherence, exchange and substitution. Second, he foresees contemporary society's central paradox, instant connectivity through a technology that simultaneously offers anonymity and encourages isolation. Finally, Williams establishes a plan of action for overcoming this central paradox by raising awareness of the energy, interconnectedness and inexhaustibility of creation's divine source. As a result, his work is clearly relevant to the current political, social and economic state of affairs.

In 1983, Alice Mary Hadfield, colleague, confidante and friend of Charles Williams, published her book, *Charles Williams: An Explanation of His Life and Work*, which is still considered a definitive study, though somewhat outdated by today's standards. There was a brief revival of interest in him in the 1990s in the aftermath of the centennial of his birth. Works published during that era by such authors as David Llewelyn Dodds, Roma A. King, Jr., and Joe McClatchey built upon and expanded Hadfield's insights. Nevertheless, with the exception of one specific collection of Charles Williams' essays, *The Image of the City* (2007), brilliantly introduced by Anne Ridler, no one author has captured the essence of Charles Williams, or the principles upon which his works were based, better than Hadfield.

Explaining the foundations of Williams' works, Hadfield inadvertently clarified the implied concept of a "good community," an interpretative category unknown to Williams in his day, but certainly applicable to his image of the "Co-inherent City." In doing so, she again unintentionally explained how his principles, outlined over seventy years ago, could resolve today's paradox of instant communication and simultaneous isolation. Just how did Williams envision the anachronous "good community"?

He developed the concept of co-inherence and its underlying principles of substitution and exchange, both being actualizations of the co-inherent life. Further, Williams, a devout Christian, saw his ideas as applicable to all humankind, regardless of religious belief or lack thereof, and "not only as operating between the living in time and space, but also between the living and the dead and the living and the unborn."[14]

One way of achieving co-inherence is through substitution, the taking up of another's burden through love, a concept expressed in St. Paul's Epistle to the Galatians 6:2. With love, one can take up another's fear, anxiety and worry. A person may take up the cross of another, because, as a member of Christ's life, one can exercise the gift and power of substitution. Just as Christ substituted himself on the cross for the transgressions of all people, in view of the fact that He had the gift of unity or co-inherence with the Father and the Holy Spirit, humans can substitute for others by taking up the others' burdens. This is a fundamental idea in all of Charles Williams' writings.

A second approach toward co-inherence is the principle of exchange. Humans are conceived through the process of exchange. Upon birth, the process continues in interactions throughout a lifetime. Alice Mary Hadfield echoes Williams' concept:

> The whole natural and social life of the world works as a process of living with each other, for good or bad: we could not be born without physical exchange, and we cannot live without it… we can each day choose or grudge it, in personal contacts, in neighbourhood, and in our society under the law. In the practice of this approach to co-inherence, we can find strength in the risen power of Christ linking all men.[15]

Thus the risen Christ becomes the interconnection and unifying force of all in the universe.

This leads to Williams' foundational concept of co-inherence. Although substitution and exchange are avenues for achieving co-inherence, they do not represent Williams' essential vision of the unity of all people in the Incarnate Christ. That role falls to co-inherence. Williams believed humans must accept that Christ sacrificed His life for us and, because He rose from the dead, His risen life exists in each one of us. Men and women share in this incarnate and redemptive act of Christ and therefore, through Jesus Christ we experience the divine co-inherence of the Holy Trinity. The action of Christ enables us to live as members within one another without being self-conscious. We are not divided from each other or from God by our degrees of intelligence, power, love or suffering, for, just as Christ's nature cannot be divided, we are all one within that nature. In Charles Williams' poem, "The Founding of the Company," he expresses this affirmation as follows:

> Terrible and lovely is the general substitution of souls
> The Flesh-taking ordained for its mortal images
> In its first creation, and now in Its sublime self
> Shows, since It deigned to be dead in the stead of each man.[16]

As Charles Williams' web of co-inherence, based upon substitution and exchange, circulated among his literary colleagues and social associates, the potential of these ideas began to emerge. Williams had struck a chord for interconnectedness in an otherwise alienated society. On the eve of World War II, this alienation was experienced not only by individuals, but also by nations, religions and atheists alike. His ideas were not considered utopian but rather very achievable with principles that were realistic and could be implemented, as he had demonstrated and would continue to demonstrate over and over again in his poetry and fiction.

More and more friends began to pressure him to create an Order of Co-inherence, or Company of Companions, centered on his ideas of co-inherence, substitution and exchange. With sincere and characteristic humility, he refused to follow this course of action for three years. However, realizing that this might be a perfect time, historically, for achieving his ideal, Williams, at last, accepted that his outline for achieving the "Co-inherent City" might be worthy of consideration as more than mere principle.

Consequently, Williams developed seven affirmations as the basis for the Order. First and foremost the Order was to have no constitution except its members. Nevertheless, the Order recommended that its members make a formal act of union with it and a formal act of recognition of their own nature's spiritual affinity with the Divine. Its concern was to be the practice of the apprehension of co-inherence both as a natural and a supernatural principle. Therefore, *per necessitatem*, the Order was Christian. Moreover, it recommends the study, on the contemplative side, of the co-inherence of the Holy and Blessed Trinity, of the Two Natures in the Single Person, of the Mother and Son, of the communicated Eucharist, and of the whole Catholic Church; *and on the active side, of Methods of Exchange in the State, in all forms of love, and in all natural things, such as childbirth* [emphasis mine]. It concludes in the Divine Substitution of Messiahs all forms of exchange and substitution, and it invokes this act as the root of all. Finally, the Order will associate itself primarily with four feasts: the Feast of the Annunciation, the Feast of the Blessed Trinity, the Feast of the Transfiguration, and the Commemoration of All Souls.[17]

Thus it was, on the eve of World War II's singularly isolating experience, Charles Williams laid out a blueprint for the unity of all humanity within the Divine's creation, and echoed the inspiration for a plan by which communication could be opened and isolation set aside for current and future generations.

Williams, therefore, was as relevant as he was significant, because his blueprint applies to the central paradox of our times as well: a technology that creates instant communication and simultaneous isolation. Furthermore, his fundamental ideas, placed in written form in 1938 with his seven principles for an Order of Co-inherence, are as applicable to our current perplexities at the beginning of the twenty-first century as are the Ten Commandments for all eternity. For the remainder of his life, he would explicate his principles in his best writing, which still lay before him until his abrupt and unexpected death in 1945.

Between 1930 and 1944, Charles Williams produced perhaps the most modern interpretation of the Arthurian myth. This is not my opinion alone, but more importantly, it is the opinion of such noted literary critics as Richard Barber, David Llewellyn Dodds, Beverly Taylor and Elisabeth Brewer. Williams' interpretation unfolded over this fourteen-year period with the publication of three works: the novel, *War in Heaven* (1930); the first cycle of his Arthurian poetry, *Taliessin through Logres* (1938); and the publication of his second cycle, *The Region of the Summer Stars* (1944). Furthermore, as indicated by the fragments of additional Arthurian poetry that surfaced after his death in 1945, Williams intended to continue his cycle.

What is there about these works that make them modern, unique, significant, relevant and worthy of memorializing? First, Williams deemphasized the Guinevere-Lancelot affair, which, up to this point in literary history, had become the focal point of the entire mythology and the reason given for the fall of Arthur's kingdom. Instead, he chose to focus on the mythical aspects of the Grail quest as central, much as Richard Wagner had done within the domain of grand opera in the previous century. He felt that Sir Thomas Malory

(1405-1471) had missed this point, and as a result, had underestimated the full potential of the myth in his *Le Morte d'Arthur*. Williams believed the quest for the Grail reflected humankind's struggle to achieve spiritual development, thus providing the quest with wider meaning, focus and centrality to the entire Arthurian myth.

These three works of Charles Williams, while covering the entire breadth of the traditional Arthurian story, made the myth into a moral epic of cosmic proportions. As a result, according to David Llewellyn Dodds, Williams' works on the Grail aspect of the myth constituted "the major imaginative work about the Grail of the Twentieth Century."[18] In addition, he clarified his concept of the "good community," an idea that is perhaps the least appreciated aspect of his view of the Arthurian story. This, then, was the "vision" of Charles Williams, a modernist view, but one that resulted in hope rather than despair. Finally, it must also be understood that at the center of Williams' vision stand two important questions. Is King Arthur there for the sake of the Grail, or is he actually secondary to the Grail and its role in the myth?

Prior to Williams' treatment, the Grail had simply been one episode in the entire mythology. Now Williams was placing the Grail at the forefront of the entire myth, a central position and the key dynamic around which his vision of the myth rotates and evolves. Williams concluded that Logres, the Welsh name Williams assigns to the more familiar Arthurian kingdom whose court centers at Camelot, exists for the Grail. This is its true glory: Arthur and Logres are meant to be players in the larger tale. For Williams, the Grail and the Quest are central to the Matter of Britain, a concept preceding even Malory, referring to the founding of the nation we know today as Great Britain.

C. S. Lewis, the foremost authority on Williams' Arthurian poetry, has stated, "We may reasonably and properly refuse this 'vision' of Charles Williams, but we can hardly doubt that, if we do so, we shall have no doubt a consistent, but a much smaller myth."[19] By using the word "consistent," Lewis is suggesting that if we place Williams' tale alongside all those that preceded his particular vision of the myth, we will see that it seems more convoluted than the others. Consequently, his tale appears to be both obscure and dense. In actuality, once we accept Williams' vision of the centrality of the Grail within the entire myth, his interpretation becomes more meaningful than obscure, more spatial than dense, more universal than limited.

Moreover, accepting the centrality of the Grail enables us to understand the myth in all its meanings, constructs and relationships. The Grail becomes the tale of Galahad and the mystical way. It is also the tale of the Way of Affirmation of Images, a sacred avenue for living and life. Williams believed that, as it enters our lives, the Grail affords us the opportunity to fulfill our spiritual destiny through co-inherence by taking up others' burdens through communion with them. Thus, we are able to fulfill the promise of the co-inherent life, a life of Trinitarian unity rather than isolation.

The Grail also becomes the tale of the universal way. Williams asserts that the Grail is the way of interconnectedness with the Magnitude existing within the universe. It is his vision of a unifying theory of the universe within a spiritual dimension. Likewise, the Grail is not only for the select; it is for all. This reinforces his concept of the interconnectedness of all humankind on every level, no matter the power, authority or station of the individual. It is the comprehension, appreciation and acceptance of this link provided by the Grail that makes for the "good community." By way of contrast, in the more traditional *Idylls of the King*, Tennyson reflects just the opposite position that the Grail is only for the elect. If we accept his interpretation, the Grail is the foundation for inequality in society, and therefore lends itself to the creation of an imperfect community.

If then the Grail is to be accepted in all the manifestations suggested by Williams, Logres must be meant as its repository. The coming of the Grail to Logres fulfills the destiny of Logres and Arthur, and the example of and the leadership for the "good community" can be realized. Anything that stands in the way of that destiny will, in the end, destroy not only the promise of Logres but also the kingship of Arthur; what evolves from that destruction is compelled to be less than it was intended to be.

Ultimately, there is one central question: whom does the Grail serve? In his book *The Holy Grail: Imagination and Belief* (2005), Richard Barber suggests that "it serves those who know its true Nature."[20] The Grail serves those who know it in all its meanings and relationships, those who, because they understand its true meaning, would lead co-inherent lives. Beverly Taylor and Elisabeth Brewer move a step beyond Barber's position in their book, *The*

Return of King Arthur: British and American Literature Since 1900 (1983), stating that "the Grail revitalizes the human spirituality of those who know its true nature."[21] This is the Grail's substantive service to humanity.

Thus the Grail serves a twofold purpose. It is the means by which the spiritual evolution of humankind can reach the ideal represented by the beatific vision of Dante's *Paradiso*. It is also the instrument through which humankind can realize its interconnectedness with the Divine, a way of co-inherence with the Infinite. This was the opportunity presented to the mythical Arthur, who in the end chose to turn from the Way of Affirmation. His human dimension overcomes his spiritual opportunity, represented by the Grail, and he fails in his leadership. The failure of Arthur's leadership must result in the failure of the kingdom to achieve its full dimensions of spirituality and complete interconnectedness with all reality within the universe.

The second purpose of the Grail is to establish Logres as the "good community." Logres shall be a place of equality, justice and the realization of interconnectedness. All these are represented through the image of the Round Table, above which the Grail will appear to those who initially are worthy of experiencing its manifestation and powers. However, when the Table is destroyed, the opportunity to experience further power is destroyed with it. From this point onward, only three great knights will be deemed deserving to seek, find and, finally, understand the true meaning of the Grail. They are Sirs Galahad, Bors and Percivale. Why these three? The answer to that will come in the ensuing chapters.

Is all hope gone? Is the promise of the Grail never to be fulfilled? Here is where the ingenuity and vision of Charles Williams truly surface. Unlike so many other modernist writers, Williams leaves us with hope, for there still remains the figure of Taliessin. He is a poet, the narrator of Williams' interpretation of the myth and our spiritual guide, much as Virgil was Dante's guide. Through the intercession of Merlin, his sister Brisen, and their mother Nimue, Taliessin understands what the Grail has to offer and does all within his power to insure the offer is acted upon.

However, working against Taliessin are forces of destruction over which he has no control. He knows and understands these forces, and while he cannot stop them, he can counteract them. Consequently, he will create a Company of Co-inherence made up of the members of his own household, and he will teach the "Way" to this Company. The Company will include the highest and lowest, as befits a true Company of Co-inherence. And, as the kingdom of Logres and the kingship of Arthur crumble, Taliessin will send out its members to teach the Way of Affirmation of Images with its principles of co-inherence, substitution and exchange. They will teach the interconnectedness of the universe's many dimensions. The Company will become Charles Williams' army of hope for the future, despite the despair of the moment.

---

[1] Jacobs 196.
[2] Jacobs 205.
[3] Seper 1.
[4] Dobson and Valentine 1.
[5] Bosky 13.
[6] Williams, *War* 139.
[7] Ibid. 139.
[8] Ibid. 140.
[9] Ibid. 141.
[10] Ibid. 141-142.
[11] Ibid. 251.
[12] "relevant," def. 2a-2b.
[13] "significant," def. 2c.
[14] Hadfield 32.
[15] Ibid. 32.
[16] Williams and Lewis, *Summer*, "The Founding of the Company" L56.
[17] Hadfield 174.
[18] Dodds 1.
[19] Williams and Lewis 267.
[20] Barber 359.
[21] Taylor and Brewer 238.

Chapter 2

War in Heaven

Charles Williams' novel *War in Heaven* was published in 1930. Though not his first novel, it was his first published novel, and as such, did not receive great acclaim. What it did do, however, was introduce Williams' interest in the Grail mythology and the concept of co-inherence. As early as 1930, no one except Williams himself had any inkling of where this interest was to lead and what the results would be.

The novel is a tale of struggle between good and evil for the Grail, the religious artifact over which these two forces battle. There are heroes and villains, and there is a child who will be the lamb to be sacrificed or saved, depending upon which of the two forces is triumphant. However, beneath this veneer lies the expression of a unique vision of the significance of the Holy Grail, not only in literature, but also as a theological symbol. Further, the novel's language itself is remarkable. Consequently, several concentric circles of Williams' reality appear: the struggle between good and evil, an interpretation of the Grail conveyed through the mythology surrounding it, and a reality articulated in the rich color of affective language.

Moreover, Williams uses *War in Heaven* to introduce the concept of co-inherence to the public. Why does he do so? Is he attempting to tap into the universal consciousness of his audience with the use of Grail mythology? Is it the means for Williams to present his theological vision of co-inherence and its spiritual expressions of substitution and exchange within his creative revelation of the Arthurian/Grail mythology? If the answer to these questions is "yes," which I believe to be the case, then Williams has begun to trace the cosmic movement of humankind toward a dynamic spiritual reality transcending time and space in the universe.

In *War in Heaven*, Williams takes ordinary people, leading otherwise ordinary lives, and confronts that normalcy with extraordinary circumstances that are both frightening and challenging, thus providing the characters with significant choices. The choices result in either spiritual life or spiritual death and are a consequence of the exercise of free will.

He begins with what his good friend, C. S. Lewis, would call a "supposal." Let us suppose a religious artifact of great import were suddenly discovered in an ordinary English parish church in a town called Fardles. It is a curious name that a playful Williams informs us is derived from the original Roman name, *Castra Parvulorum*, the Camp of the Children. He explains:

> The Castra was dropped, and in *parvulorum* the "p" became "f" and the "v" became "d." And Grimm [Jakob Grimm, 1785-1863, German philologist and folklorist] discovered what had happened. But I [the Archdeacon] try and keep the old name as well as I can. It's not far from London. They say Caesar gave it the name because his soldiers caught a lot of British children there, and he sent them back to their own people.[1]

But to return to the religious artifact: the questions inferred must be, what would be the effect on the lives of those directly or indirectly associated with this knowledge, and what if that religious artifact were none other than the Holy Grail of Arthurian mythology? Williams concludes that a struggle must ensue. The forces of evil are represented by the characters of George Persimmons, a publisher consumed by the occult; Manasseh, whom Williams describes as a master of the occult; and Dimitri, whom Williams identifies as a disciple of Manasseh. These must possess the Grail in order to destroy it. This is their mission and vocation, to destroy whatever may be good in the world.

On the other hand, the forces for good are represented by three characters. The Archdeacon Julian Davenant, pastor of the Fardles church and the embodiment of Williams' concept of co-inherence, is the first. He understands the author's frequently quoted phrase, "This also is Thou, neither is this Thou." In the *Arthurian Torso*, C. S. Lewis states:

Two spiritual maxims were constantly present to the mind of Charles Williams: 'This also is Thou' and 'Neither is this Thou.' Holding the first we see that every created thing is, in its degree, an image of God, and the ordinate and faithful appreciation of that thing a clue, which, truly followed, will lead back to Him. Holding the second we see that every created thing, the highest devotion to moral duty, the purest conjugal love, the saint and the seraph, is no more than an image, that every one of them, followed for its own sake and isolated from its source, becomes an idol whose service is damnation. The first maxim is the formula of the Romantic Way, the 'affirmation of images' [Dante's Via Positiva]: the second is that of the Ascetic Way, 'the rejection of images' [Dante's Via Negativa]. Every soul must in some sense follow both. The Ascetic must honour marriage and poetry and wine and the face of nature even while he rejects them; the Romantic must remember even in his Beatrician moment 'Neither is this Thou.'[2]

Davenant knows that the Grail must be protected for what it represents, but that it is only a pointer to a much higher expectation. For the sake of the paschal lamb, the child Adrian, he will sacrifice his own existence as a substitution in the concluding chapter of the novel. The Archdeacon's associates are a Roman Catholic aristocrat, the Duke of North Ridings, and a publisher's clerk at the Persimmons firm, Kenneth Mornington. Each will support the Archdeacon in his effort to maintain the spiritual and physical integrity of the Grail, while Mornington will sacrifice his life on its behalf.

In paralleling the Grail mythology and in an effort to reinforce the significance of that mythology, Williams has Mornington state the following during a car chase in which the three knights are attempting to save the Grail from falling into the hands of the evil force, represented by Gregory Persimmons.

> "We're carrying the San Graal,… Lancelot and Pellas and Pellinore—no, that's not right—Bors and Percivale and Galahad. The Archdeacon's Galahad, I'm Bors—but I'm not married either, and Bors was. It doesn't matter; [turning to the Duke] you must be Percivale, because you're a poet. And Bors was an ordinary workaday fellow like me. On, on to Sarras!"

He looked back over his shoulder. "Sarras!" he cried to the car behind. "We shall meet at Carbonek."[3]

How does Charles Williams present his vision of "good" and "evil"? How can he describe what for him was a vivid reality, a reality we would not be capable of fully comprehending unless confronted by a verbal account of graphic detail? It was important for Williams to communicate the horror of evil, which he knew to exist as a real force in the world. Only in confronting the existence of evil, can we appreciate the reality of Williams' "good." To achieve his purpose, Williams juxtaposes two significant events.

In chapter seven, Gregory Persimmons and his associates have gained temporary possession of the Grail. Their purpose is to use it to gain power over the innocent child, Adrian, whom Persimmons intends to make an oblation to the deity of evil they worship obsequiously. In a reenactment of a Black Mass, Persimmons stretches his hands over the Grail and utters the Latin words:

> *Pater Noster, qui fuisti in caelis… per te omnipotentem in saecula saeculorum… hoc est calix, hoc est sanguis tuus infernorum… in te regnum mortis, in te delectation corruptionis, in te via et vita scientiae malefica… qui non es in initio, qui eris in sempiternum. Amen.* "Our Father, who were in the heavens… through all-powerful you into the… this is the goblet, this is your blood of infernal beings… in you (is) the kingdom of death, in you the pleasure of corruption, in you the way and the life of evil knowledge… he who is not in the beginning, you who will be into the everlasting. Amen."…
> *De corpora, de mente… mitte animum in simulacro… per potestatem tuam in omnibus… animum Adriani cujus nomen scripsi in sanguine meo dimitte in sanguine tuo… Adrianum oblationem pro me et pro seipsum… nomen tuum.* "From the body, from the mind… send a spirit in the likeness… through your power in all things… send down in your blood the spirit of Adrian whose name I wrote in blood… Adrian the offering on behalf of me and on behalf of he himself… your name."… *De Cujus corpora haec sunt… O Pater, O Pater, O Nox et Lux infernorum et domus rejectionis.* "From whose body these things are… O Shepherd, O Father, O Night and Light of infernal beings and home of repulsion."…
> *Adrianum filium tuum, ovem tuam… et omnia opera mea et sua… tu cujus sum et cujus erit… dimitte… dimitte.* "Your son Adrian, your egg… and all my and his labors… you whose I am and whose

he will be… send down… send down."… Adrian, it is I who speak, image to image, through this shadow of thee to thee. Adrian, well met. Know me again, O soul, and know me thy friend and master. In the world of flesh know me, in the world of shadows, and in the world of our lord. Many times I shall shape thy image thus, O child, my sacrifice and my oblation, and thou shalt come, more swiftly and more truly thou, when I desire thee. Image of Adrian, dissolve and return to Adrian, and may his soul and body, whence thou hast come, receive this message that thou bearest. I, *dismissus es.*'… *Hic in me et ego in hoc et Tu, Pastor et Dominus, in utrisque.* "He is in me and I am in him and You, Shepherd and Master, are in each."[4]

What is missing in this graphic portrayal of the practice of evil? What has Williams deliberately omitted from the scene in which we see the offering of the soul of a child to the core of hell? It is *agape*—love—the love of the Light whose foundation is hope: perfect love, by which one sublimates one's own ego willingly and without reservation to the ego of the Beloved, knowing full well that the Beloved infuses the lover with a state of perfect unity and grace. Only through perfect love can Williams' state of co-inherence be achieved. In a state of co-inherence, one will not hesitate to take up the burden of another through substitution or exchange. This is the meaning of love for Charles Williams. Nowhere does its expression manifest itself in the former scene. What emerges is a distortion of that love which emanates from the center of the Grail. It is a perspective that cries out "love me and despair." The power that exists in the center of the true Grail is the sacrifice on the cross of the Incarnate One. This sacrifice, made out of perfect love and expressed through the wine, water and bread, has accomplished humankind's redemption.

Instead of pure love, the absence of the willingness to sacrifice anything but the soul of a young child looms large. There is no hope, only the abomination of the concept of love, and there is despair. Though not immediately apparent, close reading of the text also demonstrates a deceitful dimension that is the environment of evil. The co-inherent state cannot root in this contaminated field. As a result, there can be no willingness to accept another's burden, no exercise of substitution and exchange. The attempt to offer an oblation of a child's soul to the darkness of nothingness can only be a heinous blasphemy. As such, this is the breeding ground for utter despair and alienation from any possibility of pure love. In this scene, Charles Williams has established his vision of evil against which he contrasts his vision of good.

In the last chapter of *War in Heaven, Castra Parvulorum* [Camp of the Children], Williams confronts his readers with the striking disparity between the evil in chapter seven's Black Mass and the glory and grace the Grail Mass offers. In fact, he uses the Grail Mass to express his personal vision of Dante's beatific light, the vision of perfect love, truth and beauty. It is witnessed by the co-inherent characters of the novel at the celebration of a Grail Mass presided over by Prester John, a legendary medieval Christian priest and warrior believed to have ruled a Christian kingdom in the Far East or Ethiopia. To the mass come those deemed worthy of what they are about to witness. They know the meaning of the Grail in all its manifestations. For them, it is the Way of Affirmation, the way of Galahad, the way of unity with the beatific light. They understand the Grail as the representation of their salvation, for the organic reality of the Incarnation lies at its center along with the concomitant experiences of the Crucifixion and the Resurrection.

Before the liturgy, Williams establishes the significance of what is about to occur by introducing Prester John:

> "I am John," a voice sounded, "and I am the prophecy of the things that are to be and are. You, who have sought the centre of the Grail, behold through me that which you seek, receive from me that which you are. He that is righteous, let him be righteous still; he that is filthy, let him be filthy still… I am sacrifice to him that hath offered sacrifice. Friend to my friends and lover to my lovers, I will quit all things, for I am myself and I am He that sent me. This war [the struggle between good and evil for control of the Grail] is ended… ."[5]

Subsequently, in describing the Grail Mass itself, Williams exposes a fragment of his understanding of the eternal with the visionary and spiritually driven prose for which he was so admired by colleagues and contemporaries, and which resonated so deeply with me:

He stood; He moved His hands. As if in benediction He moved them, and at once the golden halo that had hung all this while over the Grail dissolved and dilated into spreading colour; and at once life leapt in all those who watched, and filled and flooded and exalted them. "Let us make man," He sang, "in Our image, after Our likeness," and all the church of visible and invisible presences answered with a roar: "In the image of God created He him: male and female created He them." All things began again to be. At a great distance Lionel and Barbara [the parents of Adrian] and the Duke saw beyond Him, as he lifted the Graal, the moving universe of stars, and then one flying planet, and then fields and rooms and a thousand remembered places, and all in light and darkness and peace. [These seemingly incongruous images evidence the interconnectedness of all within the universe, an essential element for understanding Williams' vision.]

He seemed to hold the Graal no more; the divine colour that had moved in that vision of creation swathed Him as a close-bound robe. Beyond Him the church was again visible, and silence succeeded to the flying music that had accompanied the vision. Like the centre of that silence, they heard His voice calling as if he called a name. He had not turned; still he faced that altar, and thrice He called and was still. [Unlike the Apostle Peter, Julian Davenant will accept his burden without fear or trepidation]. The Archdeacon stood up suddenly in his stall; then he came sedately from it, and turned in the middle of the chancel to face the three who watched. He smiled at them, and made a motion of farewell with his hand; then he turned and went up to the sanctuary. At the same moment Adrian [the child of four], as if in obedience to some command, scrambled to his feet and came down towards his mother. At the gate of the sanctuary the two met; the child paused and raised his face; gravely they exchanged the kiss of peace. Before Adrian had reached Barbara, the other began to mount the steps of the altar and, as he set foot on the first, sank gently to the ground.

On the instant, as they gazed, the church, but for them and the prostrate form, was empty. The sunlight shone upon an altar as bare as the pavement before it; without violence, without parting, the Graal and its Lord were gone.

    They knelt and prayed, and only stirred at last when, with the natural boredom of childhood, Adrian said in a minute to his mother; "Shall we go home?" The words dissolved as by a predestined act of the forces that held them.[6]

With two contrasting scenes, Williams reveals his vision of good and evil. While the Black Mass is an example of an impure love that can only result in despair and alienation, the Grail Mass is starkly contrary. The Black Mass declares "love me and despair." The Grail Mass affirms "love Me and hope." Thus Williams presents two ends of the spectrum of love; despair and hope.

What is truly intriguing about the Grail Mass is the company of characters in attendance. Here Prester John represents the Incarnate Truth. He is not only the spiritual protector of the Grail; he is also the organic representative of the Grail's mystery and power contained within its center.

The attendant at the service is Adrian. No longer in danger of becoming an oblation to evil, he is now quite capable, even at the age of four, of attending to the needs of the celebrant. He lives in innocent spirituality, which only the youngest of the flock can know. Consequently, he is the only presence pure enough to serve the Grail, its protector and the Incarnate Word.

The Archdeacon has fulfilled his destiny. With spiritual strength and unshakeable confidence, he has protected a chalice, which may or may not be the Holy Grail, but which, in any case, he has determined is a pointer to the Divine Mercy. Thus, he is Galahad bearing the mystery of his faith to Sarras. His spirituality is such that he will make the ultimate sacrifice for his belief by offering his life in exchange for Adrian's life. His exchange will be without reservation and filled with love, for he is the greatest knight of this small fellowship.

The Duke of North Ridings is this company's poet. Through his imagination, readers witness the little church filled with the spirits of those who were and are. He hears their voices raised in adulation for the celebration that is taking place, and he sees the forms of the voices all about the church. He experiences and remembers all. Perhaps he will later transcribe this scene in the lyrical voice of the sacred muse.

Finally, there are Barbara and Lionel Rackstraw, Adrian's parents. Because of Gregory Persimmons' machinations, they have gone through their own hell. Barbara has been to the abyss; however, as a result of her husband's love and the love of devoted friends, she has survived. Out of their physical and spiritual confrontation with this evil, Barbara and Lionel have renewed their holy and spiritual love for each other beyond any measure designed by man. It is complete.

Before our very eyes, Williams has created a co-inherent company, demonstrating the unified spiritual power of a small coterie of likeminded individuals in the face of the most overwhelming evil. Yet, the members of this company are only ordinary people, confronted by extraordinary circumstances. Through them, Williams has shown us how to overcome despair and alienation, and how to replace these with hope. Each of the characters in this final scene draws strength from the others by bearing one another's burdens. The result has been a spiritual triumph which none could achieve as individuals. Their fellowship is coalesced in the Grail Mass, and Lionel, Barbara and the Duke shall, as a result, witness the living universe and the unity of all within that universe in "light and darkness and peace."[7] With an inner quiet, they have listened and heard the words of the angelic messengers of the Incarnate Word.

In *The Novels of Charles Williams,* Thomas Howard states:

> It is as though a Cloud of Glory, like the cloud that accompanied Israel in the wilderness, has come very close to the characters in this tale and then has passed on its way, leaving them chastened, sobered, even transfigured. And this, of course, is exactly what any experience ought to convey to us in any case, Williams always implies. The mass, since it is the exact diagram of how that [sacramental and eternal] Glory touches our ordinary experiences, is an appropriate climax to the events we have witnessed in *War in Heaven.*[8]

With this first published novel, Charles Williams established the foundation for the calculus he would develop in his future novels and poetry. There is an intrusion upon the lives of ordinary people, an ensuing struggle between good and evil and, finally, the gathering of the strength to conquer the evil through the embracing of co-inherence's quintessence. One or several of the characters will take up burdens, because only through the acceptance of another's burden by the exercise of free will can the pure love of the co-inherent concept and company be achieved. With the utilization of substitution and exchange, one can begin to savor the co-inherence of the Trinity, the actuality of the sacrifice of the cross, and the promise rendered by the Incarnation of the Divine Mercy in human flesh. Consequently, Williams establishes a pattern based upon a theological belief that will become the foundation for all his subsequent novels and poetry. Perhaps his friend, Owen Barfield, sums up this point most clearly in a brief but eloquent commentary on *War in Heaven,* appearing on the back cover of the Eerdman edition of the novel. "Charles Williams' firm conviction that the spiritual world is not simply a parallel with that of the material, but is rather its source and abiding infrastructure, is explicit in both the manner and matter of all he wrote."

War in Heaven is part detective story, part supernatural thriller: a suspense novel about relationships, self-growth, spiritual search and discovery, but not in a traditional sense. Williams is in fact a literary alchemist who transmutes what seems the reality of the material world by passing the reader through portals of time and space until the mind begins to grasp the interconnectedness of all within the universe. In his article, "War in Heaven by Charles Williams," Jon Boyd states that

> the juxtaposition of holy mysticism with black magic in this story—which sets them together in the plot but stands well clear of combining or confusing them… [permits Williams to] show us characters who are engaged in mortal combat whose stakes are high and whose outcome is in real doubt, but he avoids buying into the modernist assumption that there's no real difference, but merely a contest between good and evil since power is all that could possibly be at stake. Nor, on the other hand, does he depict good and evil as deadlocked in a Manichean stalemate.[9]

Some sixty years after his death, Charles Williams' work still provokes interest in what he has to offer. There are those who will pick up his work and, after a few pages, throw down his novel or poetry in total disgust and confusion. And yet, there are many others who feel compelled to pay attention and are even in awe of his creative efforts. Why is this so?

Thomas Howard suggests that it is the sheer force of Williams' imagination and the energy he brings to his writing that drives readers to pay close attention.

> It must somehow crowd you along towards real significance. Your surprise must turn out to be recognition… This is true. Why haven't I seen this all along? What could be more obvious? What could be more lucid? … . We are startled awake by the sheer color and brilliance of the imagery, but we are shaken when we see the distance between that imagery and our own experience dwindle… The vision rushes at us… and envelops the subdued colors of commonplace experience, suffusing it all with incandescence… . For the moment it does seem that Byzantium is very near.[10]

As demonstrated in this first novel, Charles Williams is a special and non-traditional writer. He is definitely not a master of English prose in the same way as are Charles Dickens and Anthony Trollope in the nineteenth century or Graham Greene and Evelyn Waugh in the twentieth century; they showed us that their world was really quite similar to ours. However, Williams shows us his world is quite different from anything we have experienced in ours. Once again, Thomas Howard points out that, although the

> question of his idiosyncratic religious vision [expressed in *War in Heaven*, his other novels and especially his poetry] does account for some of the difficulty that might stand in the way of his being taken seriously by modern criticism… technically his religious vision was not idiosyncratic. It was a matter of traditionally Christian orthodoxy. But his way of picturing it was emphatically idiosyncratic.[11]

Howard goes on to add:

> Williams extols a whole fabric of things that appear incredible to our epoch… quaint… less than serious… his presuppositions are remote from contemporary sensibility… [however] he obliges us to keep saying, this is Williams—this is Williams.[12]

In conclusion, Charles Williams demonstrates the dramatic differences between our unimaginative vision of the world and his transcendental vision of the same world. And with his creative interpretation and implementation of the Holy Grail's mythology he presents one of the clearest explanations of faith as the "substance of things to be hoped for." He offers humankind a strong message of hope through the Divine Mercy's reality and ecumenical Christianity's actualization.

---

[1] Williams, *War* 24.
[2] Williams and Lewis 335.
[3] Williams, *War* 120.
[4] Ibid. 92-93.
[5] Ibid. 245-246.
[6] Ibid. 254-255.
[7] Ibid. 255.
[8] Howard 107.
[9] Boyd 2.
[10] Howard 297.
[11] Ibid. 294.
[12] Ibid. 294-296.

Chapter 3

Charles Williams' Arthuriad

Those who read the Arthuriad of Charles Williams must suspend their own perception of reality and enter into the poet's imagination and vision, since he creates a completely new interpretation of the original Arthurian myth in which the Grail and Galahad are central. They are symbols shared within the pattern of our collective unconscious.

However, are we as familiar with the myth, the Grail and Galahad, as we think we are? Williams asks us to reconsider their roles by thrusting the myth into a new dimension, where the Grail and Galahad are the central dynamic forces. There is also the character of the poet, Taliessin, to be treated as a pivotal focal point. We must ask ourselves, "What is his role in this new and creative interpretation?"

Malory deals with the Grail in only one chapter of his *Le Morte d'Arthur*. For Charles Williams that was not enough. He believed that the Grail must be central, because it was the source of connection with the organic Christ. Williams concluded that if this were so, must it not therefore logically be a source for humankind's redemption and grace?

In the early thirteenth century, Cistercian monks, who were at the forefront of the Reform movement of that era, rewrote the entire story of Arthur to present a counterpoint to the earlier version, which had celebrated courtly love and its subsequent sexual sub-context. In doing so, the monks created what came to be known as the Vulgate Cycle, which is a series of five interrelated books retelling the entire Arthurian saga in the form best known today.[1] The cycle bears out both Cistercian ingenuity and the figure and symbol of Galahad. No character within the western literary galaxy can match his spiritual persona, dramatic significance, or continued endurance.

If Galahad is the gift of the Cistercians to Arthurian mythology, is not Taliessin Charles Williams' gift? He takes the historical figure of an early and obscure Welsh poet and successfully transforms him into an unparalleled literary character who plays important roles. First, he serves as Williams' counterpart to Dante by narrating as the astute observer. His eyes witness and describe the destruction of Logres in the Matter of Britain. Ultimately, he inspires the continuation of the Galahadian ideal. And finally, he represents the alter ego of the poet himself.

The analysis of Charles Williams' Arthuriad requires a systematic approach that provides a rationale, an explanation for the choice of specific poems, their arrangement into categories, and the titles of those categories, with each representing a separate chapter. A singular hierarchy of the dynamic factors in the Arthuriad serves as the foundation for the entire approach.

This study attempts to trace Charles Williams' unique interpretation of the Grail Quest's mythology and his matchless capabilities as a poet/writer. For Williams, the quest for the Grail was a metaphor for humanity's cosmic spiritual journey from the Fall of Adam to the Redemption of the Cross. It is also Williams' metaphoric vision of what might have been, had there been no Fall by Adam, and what may still be. In addition, it illustrates Williams' literary inventiveness and challenges his threatened obscurity.

To make the Arthuriad more understandable for a wider audience, C. S. Lewis suggested a certain sequence for reading the poems based upon the chronological history of Arthur and his court. This study follows Lewis' sequence, but with certain significant differences. To better illustrate the cosmic spiritual experience expressed in the poems, Williams groups them into four categories, similar to those Lewis established; however, the titles are more representative of each category's focus. Moreover, in light of a hierarchical construct explained later in this chapter, the study examines seventeen specific poems in the cycle, rather than all thirty-two. The poems chosen constitute a concise logical sequence in tracing Williams' metaphor of the Fall to the Redemption.

The following four groupings of poems follow the hierarchy identified above. The hierarchy itself will subsequently be investigated in greater detail.

The first grouping identifies the poems contained in chapter four, "The Empire Ascendant: Revealing Possibilities." The three poems examined are: "Prelude," "The Calling of Taliessin," and "The Vision of Empire."

The "Prelude" and "The Calling" are from the *Region of the Summer Stars* and "The Vision" is from *Taliessin through Logres*. These specific poems are grouped in the first category because they express three significant foundations of the Arthuriad: the doctrine of largesse, Taliessin's experience with the interconnection of all in the universe, and the cosmic spiritual eloquence of the Trinity. The latter two elements also illustrate the concept of co-inherence.

The second grouping identifies the poems examined in chapter five, "Auroral Logres: Possibilities of Brilliant Splendor." The poems are: "Taliessin's Song of the Unicorn," "Bors to Elayne: The Fish of Broceliande," "Taliessin on the Death of Virgil," "The Founding of the Company," and "The Departure of Dindrane."

As Logres is ablaze with the brilliance of the aurora borealis in the northern night skies, the possibilities seem endless. "The Unicorn," "The Fish of Broceliande," and "Virgil" are from *Taliessin through Logres*, while "The Founding" and "Dindrane" are from *The Region of the Summer Stars*. The latter two poems are found in C. S. Lewis' third grouping of the cycle. Here, they appear in the second category because they, along with the other three poems in this category, deal with a second rank of Williams' foundational concepts and the possibilities that lie before Logres. They illustrate the Doctrine of Love from two perspectives: Charles Williams' theology of substitution and exchange, and the ideas of excellent absurdity and the fullness of grace.

The third grouping consists of the poems examined in chapter six, "The Uncoupling of Empire: The Seeds of Destruction." The poems are: "The Crowning of Arthur," "Lamorack and the Queen Morgause of Orkney," "Bors to Elayne: on the King's Coins," and "Taliessin in the Rose Garden."

The Uncoupling of Empire begins with "The Crowning" from *Taliessin through Logres*. The poem appears here, rather than in the first category as Lewis elects, because it reveals a major impediment leading to the ultimate destruction of Logres, the emerging egotism of Arthur. "Lamorack" and "The King's Coins," both from *Taliessin through Logres*, draw together in one vision all the evils and threats of evil existent in Logres. They also illustrate C. S. Lewis' point of view that "evil is not imperfection, nor is it revolt, but rather, miscreation, and, as such, an offense against the principle of Exchange."[2] As a result, it must foil the work of the Grail. Finally, "The Rose Garden," from *The Region of the Summer Stars*, defines Guinevere as another important element in the failure of Logres.

The final grouping of poems is examined in chapter seven, "The Galahadian Ideal: Redemption Triumphant." The poems examined are: "The Son of Lancelot," "The Coming of Galahad," "Percivale at Carbonek," The Last Voyage," and "Taliessin at Lancelot's Mass."

Five poems in the last category are from *Taliessin through Logres*. Williams' cycle turns on "The Son" and "The Coming of Galahad." Galahad is the one most worthy of imitation with the potential of achieving redemption for the whole. His birth signifies that all that has gone before will now attain perfection. Moreover, Galahad's birth allows the fulfillment of the Quest. "Percivale at Carbonek" illustrates Williams' unique vision and practice of literary alchemy. "The Last Voyage" presents Williams' perception of universal reconciliation. Finally, Taliessin's company remains to carry this message of hope. The concluding poem, "Lancelot's Mass," clarifies and actualizes universal forgiveness, exchange and reconciliation.

Charles Williams' Arthuriad revolves around an axis consisting of eight specific dynamic factors, ordered in a hierarchy of importance. Remove any one, and the power and energy of the cycle begins to crumble. Moreover, the essence of his vision becomes opaque. Precise definitions of each factor identified can be found in Paul J. Spaeth's *Charles Williams (1886-1945) Taliessin Terms*.

Descending from the apogee of terms to the base of the hierarchy, the most important is the Holy Grail. It is symbolic of the Second Coming and is capable of uniting the religious ideals of Christianity with the worldly ideals of civilization. The Grail has the capacity to bring about the perfection of Christendom on earth. However, the striking of the dolorous blow upon King Pelles hinders the coming of the Grail. The illicit affair of Guinevere and Lancelot and the begetting of Modred through the incestuous rendezvous of Arthur and Morgause further hinder the implementation of the Grail's gifts.[3]

On the next level of the hierarchy stand Byzantium and Sarras. Byzantium is the fullest realization of co-inherence encapsulated within Williams' idea of the City. It is the central unity of which all creation is an infinite variation. This poetic symbol represents the earth.⁴ In comparison, Sarras is co-inherence itself and heaven on earth, because it is the land of the Trinity, the heavenly city, and it is to Sarras that Galahad, Percivale and Bors will travel in completion of their quest for the Grail, bearing the body of Percivale's sister, Dindrane, for burial there.⁵

Carbonek, just beneath Byzantium and Sarras, is the connecting place between the earthly heaven of Sarras and the organic reality of Byzantium. Home to the wounded King Pelles and his daughter, Elayne, the mother of Galahad, it is also where the Holy Grail and the Sacred Spear of Longinus rest; the place where Percivale fails to ask the question that would have healed the wound of King Pelles, thus preventing the collapse of Logres.⁶

Following Carbonek, Taliessin and Galahad are co-players in Williams' poetic drama. Taliessin, the court poet, serves as Williams' alter ego. As such, he is the enabler and narrator of the Arthuriad, empowered to see and experience everything that is taking place. He peels back the Arthuriad's skin layer by layer and explores the matter's central core.

By comparison, Galahad, the central figure of the entire Arthuriad, accomplishes the union between heaven and earth. His birth represents the turning point. He provides the means of redemption through his saintly persona and his capacity to unveil the Grail. Only he understands the mystery that the Grail's spiritual significance lies in the reality that the organic substance of the Incarnation has been embraced within it. His spiritual awareness senses that, although the organic substance may no longer be visible in the cup, the power of that substance continues to alchemize among the unseen qualities that are the Grail.⁷

Merlin is one of the more difficult dynamic factors to define. He does not act alone, but rather, in concert with his mother, Nimue, and his sister, Brisen. Moreover, he is in the forefront of the action as he guides Taliessin at the very beginning of the cycle. In a dreamlike vision, he teaches Taliessin the purpose of the poet's existence and the possibilities that lie ahead for the kingdom of Logres. Later, Merlin protects the young baby, Galahad, as he carries the child on his back through the wintry snow from Carbonek to the protection of Dindrane's foster care. Merlin, who has taken on the form of a white wolf, is pursued by the wolverine form of the child's father, Lancelot. If he could, Lancelot would devour the child, whose birth is the source of his madness and the symbol of his infidelity with Guinevere. Despite the ferocity of the pursuit, Merlin succeeds and finally guides Taliessin in the preparation of the company to be left after the fall of Arthur's kingdom, when Logres will become Britain.

The next level of the hierarchy consists of four characters, around whose interaction much of the cycle evolves. The first of these is Arthur, who, through his acceptance of his spiritual and civil duties as king, achieves the Grail, the grace that subsequently ensues, and the realization of the greatness for which Logres is intended. However, in the midst of his moment of crowning achievement, as he accepts the mantel of investiture, the thought flashes across his mind, "the king made for the kingdom, or the kingdom made for the king?"[8] Thus, Arthur fails in this most significant of spiritual challenges in allowing his pride to overcome what should be a humbling moment in his assumption of the kingship of Logres. This act, along with the neglect of his duties as a husband, hinders the coming of the Grail, resulting in the dissolution of the kingdom.

Guinevere, Arthur's wife and queen, is involved with Lancelot in an illicit relationship, which is the central focus of many earlier renditions of Arthur and his kingdom, and an example of the sexual subtext of courtly love. However, for Williams, the focus remains the Grail. He does not ignore the reality that Guinevere's failure in her responsibilities as queen is instrumental in the kingdom's destruction, but the queen's actions are only one of the many impediments preventing the Grail from coming to Logres.

Of all the figures of the hierarchy, Lancelot is perhaps the most tragic. He is the flawed flower of Arthurian knighthood, who cannot control his desire for Guinevere and commits to a relationship that can only add to the ultimate destruction of Logres. He is deceived by the enchantress Brisen, Merlin's sister, into having intercourse with Elayne, the daughter of King Pelles. The child Galahad will be born out of this exchange. When Lancelot realizes his failure, he suffers from the guilt of betrayal of his beloved Guinevere, a fatal flaw, since, had there been no relationship with the Queen, he would have maintained his status as the preeminent flower of knighthood. The result is devolution into bestiality in the form of a wolf. Possessed by this madness, Lancelot stalks the child of his loins and seeks to devour him. Once again, Logres experiences a major incident that will contribute to its destabilization and result in its destruction.

Finally, Williams presents Dindrane. If any woman could be more of what Guinevere should be as Queen, Dindrane is that woman, as she fulfills the role of protector of the infant Galahad. She comes closest to experiencing pure platonic love with Taliessin, ultimately choosing the Way of Negation in retiring to the convent at Almesbury. However, because of her love for Taliessin, she accepts his perception of the Way of Affirmation. And Taliessin, because of his love for Dindrane, accepts her perception of the Way of Negation. Not the least of Dindrane's glory is the acquiescent exchange of her blood for that of a dying girl, resulting in her burial in the soil of holy Sarras.

The next order of the hierarchy centers on Logres. The northernmost kingdom of the majestic Empire is destined to be the perfect manifestation of the civil order and spiritual grace of that Empire, the exemplary society in reality. This can only be achieved through the arrival of the Grail. However, because of the many shortcomings of the kingdom's key characters, the Grail cannot come to Logres, which becomes only a passing realization of the ideal society it might have been.[9]

The final dynamic factor is King Pelles, also referred to as the Fisher King. He reigns over Carbonek as one of a long line of guardians of the Grail, suffering constant pain from a wound to the groin inflicted upon him by Balin with the Sacred Spear. The flow of blood from the wound, which is both physical and spiritual and a powerful metaphor for the Cross, is constant and cannot be stemmed. As a result, his physical and spiritual virility are also affected. The wound is also a symbol of the Fall and thus, both a physical and spiritual hurt suffered by all mankind. Moreover, the blood flow and constant pain are symbolic of the passion of Christ on the cross, making the character of Pelles most important as a symbolic representation of mankind's Fall, the resulting spiritual and physical hurt inflicted upon mankind, and, finally, the redemption of humankind by the passion and death of Christ on the cross. Indeed, this one figure represents the whole cosmic spiritual experience of humankind from the Fall to the Redemption. Pelles is a microcosm of Charles Williams' macrocosmic Arthurian cycle.

The hierarchy of dynamic factors dealt with in this chapter represents a particular strategy for the consideration and comprehension of Charles Williams' cycle. This skeletal structure supports an organic body consisting of the Arthuriad's seventeen most significant poems divided into four categories. To complete the anatomical metaphor, the head coincides with "The Empire Ascendant," the torso with "Auroral Logres," the limbs with the "Uncoupling of Empire," and the soul with "The Galahadian Ideal." Thus, the strategy's design is now in deliberate order.

---

[1] Pickin 1.
[2] Williams and Lewis 316.
[3] Spaeth 3.
[4] Ibid. 2.
[5] Ibid. 6.
[6] Ibid. 2.
[7] Ibid. 3.
[8] Williams and Lewis, *Taliessin*, "The Crowning of Arthur" L39
[9] Spaeth 4.

Chapter 4

The Empire Ascendant: Revealing Possibilities

Charles Williams is buried in the churchyard of the parish Church of St. Cross-Holywell in Oxford, England. The grave marker bears his name, the dates of his birth and death, and the word "Poet" inscribed within a laurel wreath; it also holds the words "Under the Mercy." If there is any clear indication available as to what the focus of his life's work was, it is contained in that word chiseled into his gravestone, "Poet." Moreover, if there is one concept within his poetry that delineates most clearly the theological focus of his poetry, it is the phrase "Under the Mercy."[1]

Charles Williams considered himself, first and foremost, a poet. He worked at poetry his entire professional life, precipitating an evolutionary growth in style, substance and personal technique that is modern and extraordinarily creative. Several noteworthy admirers, including T. S. Eliot, Dorothy Sayers, Anne Ridler, Glenn Cavaliero, and Roma E. King, Jr., agree that the culmination of his poetic efforts is best illustrated in the Arthurian cycles, *Taliessin through Logres* and *The Region of the Summer Stars*. These two cycles demonstrate Williams' poetic stature at its zenith, and in them we first encounter the meaning of the phrase "Under the Mercy," as he reveals his complex theology, ever so cleverly, through the mythological symbolism of the Holy Grail.

In his journal article "The Diagrammatized Glory of Charles Williams' *Taliessin through Logres*," Joe McClatchey states, "In *Taliessin through Logres*, Williams asks and answers the question, "What is the central myth, the genius of the Arthurian story?"[2] He is not interested in its superficialities; rather, he seeks the core of the myth, or, as McClatchey characterizes it, "the untranscendable thing."

Williams sets his tale within the historical context of the sixth-century Byzantine Empire. He then asks, "What did the mind of that world want most?" His answer is "the Parousia or Return of Christ."[3] Furthermore, if, as Williams believes, the Byzantine throne is a "worthy imperial vicar of Providence," then it is reasonable to ask, "What does the Emperor want, and subsequently, what does God want?"[4]

> According to McClatchey:
>
> The answer is the same as before: the Second Coming. But the way must be made straight, as it was for His Advent. There must be a union of the two greatest symbols of Christ: the Grail and the Throne, that is, the Eucharist and the Kingdom, the Cross and the Promised Land, the Body and the City, Carbonek and Camelot. The Geography and the Geometry require the third thing needful, the Myth, the Double-Fledged Logos—Christ Himself.[5]

Who, then, can tell the tale? It cannot simply be a retelling, the old tale revised and retold again and again. No, the Imagination works on and in and through the imagination, or, as McClatchey states:

> It comes to be, not because a story is told… but because Imagination somehow ordains it and finds an imagination that will tell it right. Imagination waits for an imagination to dare a new thing in the universe of the legends, to give the story a new orientation, to drive down a landmark in the landscape of the literature. The myth, then, is the imagination's contribution to the story and its real work. Many Arthurian tellings are called, but only myth is chosen.[6]

For McClatchey, Williams is the chosen imagination ordained by the Imagination to dare a new thing in the universe of legends.

The theological axis around which Williams' mythic cycle rotates embraces the doctrine of largesse, proclaimed through the Incarnation, the interconnection of all in the universe, manifested in creation itself and the cosmic spiritual reality of the Trinity, heralded through co-inherent relationship, one with another and also within community. The basis for these core beliefs can be traced to two documents with which Williams was not only familiar, but which were the substructures of his entire belief system.

The first is the Nicene Creed, which articulates in lines thirteen through seventeen:

> For us and for our salvation
> he came down from heaven:
> by the power of the Holy Spirit
> he became incarnate from the Virgin Mary,
> and was made man.

Is there a clearer expression of the doctrine of largesse and its origin, or the interconnection of all within the universe, than this subsequent act of procreation, the Incarnation of Jesus Christ?

The second document is the Athanasian Creed. There is no more crystalline pronouncement of the co-inherence of the Trinity and humankind's opportunity to take part in that co-inherent circumstance than in the fifth through eighth lines of this creed:

> And the Catholic Faith is this:
> That we worship one God in Trinity, and Trinity in Unity,
> neither confounding the Persons,
> nor dividing the Substance.

Furthermore, in lines thirty-nine through forty-three the creed goes on:

> But the whole three Persons are co-eternal together and co-equal.
> *So that in all things...* [emphasis mine]
> The Unity in Trinity and the Trinity in Unity is to be worshipped.
> He therefore that will be saved must think thus of the Trinity.

With this foundational structure in place, we begin to explore the poetry with which Williams articulates his Incarnational and Trinitarian theology, and we examine the dynamic factors he uses to explain that theology within the pattern of Arthur and the Holy Grail.

The Empire Ascendant: Revealing Possibilities must begin with the *Prelude* to *The Region of the Summer Stars*. Byzantium is the center of orthodox imagination. The co-inherent Trinity is apotheosized. The Emperor sits upon his throne and, symbolizing the Father, governs an empire where Civilization and the City are geometrically, geographically and physiologically congruent. The whole waits in anticipation of "the Second coming of the Union."[7] Further, the Empire ponders:

> Hope, as by the night the first of the summer stars
> in the universal sky high hung,
> in them looks on the sea, and across the sea
> saw coming, from the land of the Three-in-One,
> in a rich container, the Blood of the Deivirilis,
> communicated everywhere, but there singly borne,
> and the morn of the Trinity rising through the sea to the sun.[8]

These lines introduce several factors which are catalysts for combining Williams' own myth with the Matter of Britain: the Parousia or Second Coming, Carbonek, the Holy Trinity, the incarnated God/Man, Galahad and Sarras. The Empire is the Theotokos for the Parousia, and the Grail is the symbolic aggregate for all Williams' imagination embraces in his interpretation of the Myth.

Thus, the *Prelude* to *The Region of the Summer Stars* establishes Williams' literary locale. The Empire, Byzantium, represents the pattern of perfection that his myth seeks for Logres. Moreover, Logres is the site chosen for the Second Coming in the form of the Holy Grail. The cosmic moment is at hand; however, as humankind fell once before, presented with the same universal occurrence, will the turning away from grace happen again? If so, will the Divine Mercy intercede this time on behalf of the fallen? These are the questions that Williams raises in this *Prelude* and confronts and answers in the remainder of his Arthurian cycle.

The second poem, illustrating the ascendency theme, is *The Calling of Taliessin*. The longest poem in the entire Arthuriad, it consists of four hundred and thirty-six lines and introduces the figure of Taliessin. He is one of the two major protagonists, the other being Galahad. He is the most Christian poet of the most Christian Empire. However, as the poem opens, Taliessin is not yet cognizant of the spiritual orthodoxy which Byzantium offers "for the Lord God had not yet set him at liberty, / nor shown him the doctrine of largesse in the land of the Trinity."[9] Nevertheless, Taliessin hears rumors of orthodox Byzantium, greater than his druidic reality and capable of quenching his thirst for cosmic truth. He chooses to seek out that truth, and thus begins his journey.

During Taliessin's third day on the road, as he rides between the lawless Logres and the dark woods of Broceliande, he encounters his Virgil in the form of Merlin, who appears with his sister, Brisen. Frightened at first, Taliessin tries to comprehend the experience, asking, "Are you mortal? Are you friend? / I do not know Arthur; I go from Wye / to find beyond the sea a fact or a fable."[10]

> Merlin answered: 'A friend, mortal or immortal,
> if you choose; we bear no arms; and for harms spiritual
> we two can placably receive the Names spoken
> in Byzantium, which shall be by Thames; it is ordered that soon
> the Empire and Broceliande shall meet at Logres,
> and the Hallows be borne from Carbonek into the sun.[11]

As the day recedes into the night, Taliessin's new companions suggest it is time for sleep. Exhaustion results in fitful slumber, begetting a cosmic vision for Taliessin, in which he sees the future and his role in the unraveling mystery. "Taliessin began then to share in the doctrine of largesse / that should mark in Camelot the lovers of the king's poet."[12]

In Hefling's *Charles Williams: Essential Writings in Spirituality and Theology*, Williams defines the doctrine of largesse as follows: "To forgive and to be forgiven are the two points of holy magnificence and holy modesty; round these two centers the whole doctrine of largesse revolves." He further points out that the doctrine of largesse is a state of "sanctification in which reconciliation and fellowship find their goal and consummation."[13]

Williams illustrates these points in the following passage and, as the vision unfolds, Merlin also charges Taliessin:

> Go son of the bards; king's poet,
> go; propolitan are the porphyry chambers; see
> and know the Empire; fulfill then an errand;
> rescue the king at Mount Badon; stand by the king,
> Arthur, the king we make, until the land
> of the Trinity by a sea-coming fetch to his stair.
> Sarras is free to Carbonek, Carbonek to Camelot;
> in all categories holds the largesse of exchange,

and the sea of Broceliande enfolds the Empire.[14]

As Taliessin drifts ever deeper into slumber, he apprehends the possibilities for Arthur and Logres. In this chimerical world of intellectual perception, he stands beside the king, watching and waiting for the coming of the Trinity through Broceliande. Even more, he sees:

> the daughter of a king, holding an unseen thing
> between her hands, but over her hands a veil,
> the saffron veil of the sun itself, covered
> all; her face was pale with stress of passion
> as the ship ran—and even in a sleep within a sleep
> Taliessin trembled.[15]

Finally, there is the possibility for failure in this grand scenario. Merlin is aware that all the characters in this play are human. Though they may be chosen to fulfill certain roles, they possess free will. The Divine Mercy may offer, but it is humankind's choice to accept or reject. Thus, he offers Taliessin a contingency plan:

> If in the end anything fail of all
> purposed by our mother and the Emperor, if the term
> be held less firm in Camelot than in Carbonek,
> as well my sister and I may guess now
> and prepare the ambiguous rite for either chance
> in the kingdom of Arthur; if cease the coming from the seas
> at the evil luck of a blow dolorously struck,
> it may be that this gathering of souls, that the king's poet's
> household shall follow in Logres and Britain the spiritual roads
> that the son of Helayne shall trace westward through the trees
> of Broceliande; they who shall be called and thrilled
> by Taliessin's purchase and their own will
> from many a suburb, many a waste; say
> that they are a wonder whose origin is not known,
> they are strown with a high habit, with the doctrine of largesse,
> who in his house shall be more than the king's poet
> because of the vows they take.[16]

The Calling of Taliesin achieves several goals for Williams. We meet Taliessin, a figure crucial to the entire Arthuriad, encounter Merlin, Taliessin's Virgil on his journey of discovery, and discern a broad outline of the plan and purpose of the cycle. Moreover, we receive answers to such questions as, what is Taliessin's responsibility in the whole matter? What form will the Second Coming take? What if humankind fails once again by refusing this opportunity for perfection, as did the first parents in the Garden of Opportunity, or humankind in the Cross' gracious offering? Furthermore, Williams introduces the doctrine of largesse, key to the perfection of the Empire and indispensable to the establishment of Logres in preparation for the Parousia. He also speaks indirectly to the concept of co-inherence with concrete references to the acts of exchange and substitution. Finally, he contemplates the survival of Logres' potential through Taliessin's household, and in doing so he constitutes the fundamental principles for the good community, consequently reinforcing the revelation of possibilities as a central theme.

The last poem in this section is *The Vision of Empire*. In *The Vision*, Taliessin discovers the plan for Logres. He also uncovers the theme of the Empire's design and witnesses a series of images related to Logres. More importantly, Taliessin reflects on the interconnection of all within the Empire, or, as Roma A. King, Jr. suggests, Taliessin becomes cognizant of *The Pattern in the Web*. Consequently, he fathoms McClatchey's untranscendable thing at the Empire's core, the cosmic eloquence of the co-inherent Trinity. This is the theme of the Empire's design and the integrity he seeks in his journey.

He begins his experiences of design and integrity when, as Williams states, "Taliessin walked through the hither angels, / from the exposition of grace to the place of images."[17] In *Answers to Questions from C. S. Lewis*, Williams further explains, "[He] has gone out of the direct presence of the Emperor into the outer world, which is precisely a place of images; from the Sacred Palace to the waters of the Golden Horn, from 'God in himself' to 'God in his creatures.'"[18]

This movement, from the realm of the divine to the realm of reflections of the divine, enables Taliessin to better grasp the co-inherent nature of creation. He sees "the theme of the design of the Empire" reflective in "the scheme of Logres." There is "balance and weight, freight of government with glory."[19]

> The Table stands rigid in the king's hall,
> and over their seats the plotted arms of the soul,
> which are their feats and the whole history of Logres.

Down the imperial highroad the white nuntius rides
to heighten the hearts of Lateran, Gaul, and Logres.[20]

As Taliessin continues on his journey, his primitive druidic wisdom is challenged by the Empire's Christian doctrine. He surfeits his intellect with the milk of Gaul's breasts, indulges in the "trigonometrical milk of doctrine" and, in doing so, advances in wisdom and knowledge of the divine Trinity.

Man sucks it; his joints harden,
sucking logic, learning, law,
drawing on the breasts of intelligo and credo.[21]

Taliessin also discovers, "the dialect of Logres was an aspect of Byzantium; / the grand art was taught in the heart of the harbours of Arthur."[22] The image of the reflection of Byzantium within Logres continues, and the poetic talent of Taliessin is infused with deeper understanding and dimension.

He next encounters the key question of the poem, "What was the crossing of the will of the Emperor?"[23] With this question, he confronts the Fall in the Garden of Opportunity and, thus, the image that portends the destiny of Logres.

Adam cries out:
forked friend,
am I not too long meanly retired
in the poor space of joy's single dimension?
Does not God vision the principles at war?
Let us grow to the height of God and the Emperor:
Let us gaze, son of man, on the Acts in contention.[24]

What exactly does Adam seek? In his essay, *He Came Down from Heaven*, Williams refers to the search as "an alteration in knowledge." Moreover, Adam knows there is an alternative to the good he is graced with. What he and Eve fail to realize is that that alternative is known by the Divine in an intellectual pattern. Yet, Adam senses that to know evil will bring him into equality with the Divine. So, with his free will, he chooses to know evil, thus sharing that knowledge with the Divine. Williams states:

Man desired to know schism in the universe. It was a knowledge reserved to God; man had been warned that he could not bare [*sic*] it—'in the day that thou eatest thereof thou shalt surely die.'

A serpentine subtlety overwhelmed that statement with a grander promise—'Ye shall be as gods, knowing good and evil.'[25]

Thus, schism is introduced into the Empire and, as Taliessin understands, must be reflected in Logres. The organic unity of the whole and the interconnectedness of the mosaic shatters beneath disunities' weight: "[They] had their will; they saw; they were torn in terror."[26]

What has been unleashed is a shockingly repellent, diametric reality to Byzantium. A headless form rules a directionless P'o-lu, as Williams imagines:

> a headless figure walks in a crimson cope,
> volcanic dust blown under the moon.
> A brainless form, as of the Emperor,
> Walks, indecent hands, hidden under the cope,
> Dishallowing in that crimson the flush on the
> mounds of Caucasia.[27]

His imagination creates a scene of bestial conduct, depicting "self-absorbed masturbatory behavior."[28] In *Answers to Questions from C. S. Lewis*, Williams explains:

> Everything is parodied, and holy intellect is lost... because all capacities are reduced to a kind of sensational preoccupation with one thing, and that is why the crimson cope obscenely resembles the first high flush of Caucasian love. If one gets *fixed* on Caucasia—![29] [emphasis original]

The poem ends in a song of praise throughout the Empire. Every portion within and without is encouraged to sing the praise of their Lord and the images that reflect the glory of the Throne. The organic body is co-inherent despite P'o-lu's outrage.

Clearly, Williams outlines the Empire's geography and characteristics, especially in terms of large areas, and the complex interrelationships obtaining among them. Also, he defines the Empire's geometry. Williams treats of space and its relations, as in a painting or sculpture. Finally, he reveals the Empire's physiology, the aggregate of all its vital processes.

Moreover, he accomplishes this by employing a complex series of symbols that, rather than confusing the projection of his myth, results in an intellectual impetus with a corresponding gain in tangibility. In his essay, *The Poetic Achievement of Charles Williams*, John Heath Stubbs argues, "The mythology employed is not private, but one whose symbols have already been charged with poetic significance by tradition, in the collective consciousness, particularly of English readers."[30]

I would add the entire English speaking world, if only through exposure to plays like *Camelot*, motion pictures, such as *Camelot* and *Excalibur*, novels like T. H. White's *The Once and Future King* and, of course, Malory's *Morte d'Arthur* and Tennyson's *Idylls of the King*.

> This is the Arthurian Legend—but stripped of its original Medievalism and of the picturesque trappings, and enacted against a background which is at once that of Eternity, and of the Sixth-Century Europe in which the historical Arthur may be supposed to have lived… [presenting] a picture perhaps closer to our own time than that of any intervening period—the civilization of the Empire threatened by forces of barbarism, the rise of new phases of faith and patterns of society.[31]

The vision is fractured, humankind falls; yet, Redemption is achievable under the Divine Mercy.

The possibilities Williams discloses in the three poems are numerous and interrelated. He makes visible the design of the Empire in all its complexity, yet beautiful in its simplicity and best expressed in the Byzantine mosaic. He exposes the reader to the indispensable cosmic eloquence manifested in the co-inherent Trinity and the Trinity's consequent significance for humankind. Williams asserts that the union of Eucharist and Kingdom through the Grail and the Throne is achievable. Thus, the untranscendable is within reach. The expectation of the Parousia is attainable, with Logres as the Mary of the Second Coming. Williams reveals the potentialities of the ascendant Empire and the Empire as pattern for the kingdom.

Furthermore, he asks the question "is humankind doomed to fall again?" The Garden of Opportunity is already witness to one tragedy because of the desire for knowledge of schism in the universe. Humanity is incapable of sharing in the Divine's intellect. Tragically, their desire is only achievable through empirical exposure. Through free will's exercise, the Adam and their progeny have to die. In *He Came Down from Heaven*, Williams declares:

> Unfortunately to be as gods meant, for the Adam, to die, for to know evil, for them, was to know it not by pure intelligence but by experience. It was, precisely, to experience the opposite of good, that is the deprivation of the good, the slow destruction of the good, and of themselves with the good.[32]

Finally, Taliessin comes into focus as Williams' alter ego serving as the catalyst for his myth. Taliessin and his household appropriate the Trinitarian characteristic of co-inherence through exchange and substitution, moving from an empirical understanding to a level of intellectual apprehension. In doing so, he is able to absorb into his consciousness the co-inherent nature of reality, reflecting the cosmic Trinity. Further, he transmits this consciousness to his household. Taliessin is truly a key dynamic factor within Williams' diagrammatic representation.

---

[1] Topolewski 1.
[2] McClatchey, "Diagrammatized" 121.
[3] Ibid. 121.
[4] Ibid. 121.
[5] Ibid. 121.
[6] Ibid. 121-122.
[7] Williams and Lewis, *Summer*, "Prelude" L51-52.
[8] Ibid. L59-63.
[9] Williams and Lewis, *Summer*, "The Calling of Taliessin" L30-31.
[10] Ibid. L203-205.
[11] Ibid. L206-211.
[12] Ibid. L318-319.
[13] Hefling 189-190.
[14] Williams and Lewis, *Summer*, "Calling" L342-350.
[15] Ibid. L383-388.
[16] Ibid. L415-431.
[17] Williams and Lewis, *Taliessin*, "The Vision of Empire" L13-14.
[18] Williams, "Answers" 2.
[19] Williams and Lewis, *Taliessin*, "Vision" L49-50.
[20] Ibid. L61-65.
[21] Ibid. L66-70.
[22] Ibid. L78-79.
[23] Ibid. L100.

[24] Ibid. L103-108.
[25] Williams, *Down from Heaven* 19-20.
[26] Williams and Lewis, *Taliessin*, "Vision." L129.
[27] Ibid. L146-151.
[28] Mihal 174.
[29] Williams, "Answers" 2.
[30] Stubbs 43.
[31] Ibid. 43-44.
[32] Williams, *Down from Heaven* 20.

Chapter 5

Auroral Logres: Possibilities of Brilliant Splendor

A singular idea and driving force behind Charles Williams' literary creations is the concept of love. Could a devotee of Dante not be enthralled by this greatest gift of the Divine Mercy? He could not, because he sees love and the Divine as one and inseparable, articulated in many dimensions, with no one dimension more significant than any other. Consequently, Williams declares love as both an intellectual and empirical participation.

The Divine shares intellectual love with us through the Holy Trinity, united as One and, at the same time, a Triad of three separate and distinct natures delineated in unity. Also, there is the love communicated in the Incarnation. Through the Incarnation, humankind and the Divine become one. This oneness enables us to partake of the Trinity's co-inherence, a co-inherence that is the path for our redemption through the occasions of substitution and exchange. Just as the Incarnated One took up humankind's burdens and exchanges by embracing the rood with love, the sacrifice liberated humankind to embrace one another with love. There is also the Father's love for His creation, perhaps best visualized as incandescent rays flowing to the creation through the Son's Divine Mercy, symbolizing the stream of grace from the Creator to the created through the Son's mediation.

Empirically, unity is communicated in community. Williams' Company of Co-inherence is representative of such a community's potential, wherein individuals unite through substitution and exchange. Yet, united, they remain individuals in unity with one another, separate and singular, actualizing within one concept, the community.

Furthermore, there is the love shared between two individuals. Here is a union of mutual intimacy beyond any one-dimensional orthodoxy, for assuredly, one substitutes one's self in carrying the other's burdens, and freely exchanges the deepest emotions. Each is a mirror for the other, and the reflected image creates a Beatrician quality for and of the other. The resulting image is a catalyst to set free potentialities empowering the divinity in each.

A second idea motivating Williams' imagination is excellent absurdity. For him, grace was more than we deserve. Consequently, we are all, in essence, superfluous to the Divine's intellect. Yet, there is a certain absurdity existent in this revelation of humankind's significance in the Intellect's plan. Humankind was created by the Divine to complete the creation, and the Divine said it was good. Therefore, no matter how superfluous our existence is, we exist, in fact, at the will of the Creator. Our superfluity is conceived in the grace of the Creator, a grace, which, according to Williams, we do not deserve. This is the paradox of creation. As a result, whether in relative dignity or rank, social or official position, manner or respect, there exists an equality of being which cannot be denied or circumvented, for, as St. Paul says, "But I discipline my body and bring it into subjection, lest, when I have preached to others, I myself should become disqualified."[1]

The first poem, expressing untainted Logres' possibilities of brilliant splendor, is *Taliessin's Song of the Unicorn*. If there is one poem in the entire Arthuriad with which Williams was the least satisfied, it is the "Unicorn." In *Answers to Questions from C. S. Lewis*, he states:

> Not very good. It had originally the notion that most women prefer direct attention to indirect labour; 'the unicorn' (poetry, social things, etc.) is regarded as less attractive than the human fellow; Catallus was a kind of 'catch' for Lesbia, but she much preferred less poetry and more intercourse, so she took up with someone else. On the other hand, it is the great ideas by devotion to which we get things done. If a woman could really help poetry, poetry might say something.[2]

In one sense, this statement pays indirect homage to the accomplishment of Dante and his Beatrice. On the other hand, the unicorn, as Taliessin realizes, is never loved, because it can never fulfill the deepest desires of the one it longs for. Devotion to one's spiritual passion, poetry, virtually excludes the required total commitment to the other's human passion.

Taliessin's Song of the Unicorn explores the conflict between creativity and romantic love. The entire poem is only thirty-six lines long; nevertheless, it demonstrates Williams' attempt to understand the nature of the poet and poetry, both of which represent the unicorn. It will come to the command of the chaste flesh, yet, ironically, it is incapable of satiating her blood. The poet's fate, like the unicorn's, is to hang as a trophy over the hunter and once maiden's couch. So the unicorn and the girl seem incompatible. The gentle beast cannot submit to the other without being disloyal to creativity, while the maiden cannot submit without surfeited blood.

However, Williams considers the other possibility of creativity and romantic love as one. He states:

> yet if any [maiden], having the cunning to call the grand beast,
> the animal which is but a shade until it starts to run,
> should dare set palms on the point, twisting from the least
> to feel the sharper impress, for the thrust to stun
> her arteries into channels of tears beyond blood... .[3]

Thus, the artful maid is capable of unleashing the creativity romantic love can inspire. Williams goes on:

> through hands to heart by the horn's longing: O she
> translucent, planted with virtues, lit by throes,
> should be called the Mother of the Unicorn's Voice, men see
> her with awe, her son the new sound that goes
> surrounding the City's reach, the sound of enskied [exalted]
> shouldering shapes, and there each science disposed,
> horn-sharp, blood-deep, ocean and lightning wide,
> in her paramour's song, by intellectual nuptials unclosed.[4]

Furthermore, in *The Taliessin Poems of Charles Williams*, Alice Mary Hadfield points out:

> If a woman dared to enter into the experience of combining love, sex and poetry, she might join in both sexual exploration and attention to poetry little by little, ever increasing both in depth and commitment without dissipating or blurring by release into the act of sexual orgasm... From it would grow

(her son) poetry with a new reach and penetration such as C. W. felt the genius of great poets was seeking... [resulting in] full attention and developing comprehension of each other's thoughts, imagination and ability... not completed, ended or limited, but ever fresh, ever new.[5]

Williams concludes that creativity and romantic love need not be in conflict, for together they can inspire one another to transcendent dimensions.

The next poem in the auroral landscape continues Williams' exploration of the doctrine of love. "Bors to Elayne: The Fish of Broceliande" is a letter written by the everyman knight to his wife, centering upon his love for her. Also, Bors does not speak with the poet's voice; rather he speaks with the voice of a soldier in love with and missing his wife while away from her in performance of his duty. After being sent to the southern coast of the kingdom to supervise the frontier with Broceliande, he remembers Taliessin's song of Broceliande, which "meant all things to all men, and you to me."[6] While remembering, Bors envisions plucking a fish from a stream and placing it in Elayne's hands. The fish enters the channel of her arm and swims uncatchable to "a fathomless bottomless pool."[7]

Can the fish receive a name? Only Nimue, the mother of creation, is capable of the naming it, or a "twy-nature,"[8] a nature attuned to the union of flesh and spirit, such as the Incarnated Jesus Christ or, as Williams suggests, the light of Romantic Love, which is of Christ. "The twy-nature, then, refers both to human love and to Christ, the Word made flesh."[9] Here Williams is suggesting the important role of exchange within the entire process of creation.

Moreover, the metaphor of the fish represents several possibilities. It may refer to the early Christian outline of a fish, used as a symbol of Christ and represented in the Greek as ICHTHUS, an anagram for the letters forming the initials of the title **JESUS CHRISTOS THEOU-UIOS SOTER**, Jesus Christ Son of God Saviour.[10] Another possibility is the fish as a symbol for the male's seed, swimming to the fathomless bottomless pool of the female and, with this exchange, taking root and producing her child, poetry's creator. This latter prospect is a metaphor within a metaphor within a third metaphor. It begins with Bors' vision of a fish, symbol of Christ in the early church, entering the channel of Elayne's arm. Also, the fish is emblematic of humankind's consummated exchange in creating life. Finally, it represents the romantic love Williams perceives as indispensable to composing cosmic poetry.

With this poem, Williams explores a wide spectrum of love's potentialities, the simple longing of a soldier for his loved one and the incarnational love of Christ for his creation, the essential exchange for procreation and the romantic love inspiring artistic creativity. However, no matter the point on the spectrum, civilization and order are achieved through love's inherent capacity for growth and development.

Within the scope of Auroral Logres, *Taliessin on the Death of Virgil* continues Williams' exploration of the doctrine of love through substitution and exchange and excellent absurdity. The poem falls into two distinct divisions. The first is a vivid description of death's experience, as Virgil falls from the edge of the world, pushed into the abyss by the buttocks of his benefactor, the Emperor Augustus. The buttocks are a metaphor for life's good experiences, civility, friendship and morality. Thus, Augustus' love pushes Virgil off the edge of the world, causing him to experience the sensation of falling ever downward into despair's pit. In describing the moment of Virgil's death, Williams' vision recounts:

> He fell through his moment's infinity [death]
> (no man escapes), all the shapes of his labour,
> his infinite images, dropping pell-mell; above,
> loomed the gruesome great buttocks of Augustus his love,
> his neighbor, infinitely large, infinitely small.[11]

So we see Dante's guide spiraling ever downward, his "infinite images" in poetry seemingly "dropping pell-mell" around him, never to be recovered.

> Perpetual falling, perpetual burying,
> this was the truth of his Charon's ferrying—
> everlastingly plucked from and sucked from
> and plucked to and sucked to a grave.[12]

But does great poetry ever really die with its creator? Even though Virgil is a pagan poet, he espouses Christian ideals and values in his poetry. Do the poetry and the poet merit death and lost remembrance? Williams confronts this dilemma of Christian ideals expressed within pagan poetry, for, in the second portion of the poem, he presents an avenue for the recovery of the poet and the poetry created by the poet's imagination.

> Unborn pieties lived.
> Out of the infinity of time to that moment's infinity
> they lived, they rushed, they dived below him, they rose
> to close with his fall; all, while man is, that could
> live, and would, by his hexameters, found
> there the ground of their power, and their power's use.
> Others he saved; himself he could not save.[13]

Who are the "Unborn pieties?" They are the once and future poets, who have learned their craft at the knee of Virgil. Time cannot interfere in this intellectual exchange; rather, time is defied. It is a mere portal separating the pagan from the Christian, yet not capable of separating the immortal imagination from infinity's embrace.

Virgil has made the supreme sacrifice, forever to be duplicated in the truly co-inherent existence. "Others he saved; himself he could not save." The substitution that he offers is founded upon love, and the commitment is complete. To save one's self is substitution without love, and, therefore, meaningless. The cross without love has no consequence. The Cross with love is transcendent spirituality. Thus, in *Taliessin through Logres, The Region of the Summer Stars,* and *Arthurian Torso,* C. S. Lewis explains:

> This poet from whose work so many Christians have drawn spiritual nourishment was not himself a Christian—did not himself know the full meaning of his own poetry, for (in Keble's fine words) 'thoughts beyond their thoughts to those high bards was given.' That is the exquisite cruelty; he made honey not for himself; he helped to save others, himself he could not save.[14]

Consequently, the "exquisite cruelty" is an excellent absurdity and the "honey" that saved others is returned in kind by those he saved. "There was intervention, suspension, the net of their loves…."[15] Here is Williams' theology of substitution and exchange, but, most importantly, with love. Williams states:

> Virgil was fathered of his friends.
> He lived in their ends.
> He was set on the marble of exchange.[16]

This is far from death in the terminative sense. Rather, it is a form of eternity for poets worthy of the Divine Mercy's beneficence. Thus, the Cross' sacrifice, with its substitution and exchange rooted in love, reaches across humankind's superficial limitations of time and space, unrestrained by reality's constraints, extending into cosmic infinity and offering approbation and grace. Williams states, in *Answers to Questions from C. S. Lewis*: "[We] live now and hereafter by others."[17] Indeed love does conquer death.

Charles Williams scholars generally agree that *The Founding of the Company* holds a central place and is the most autobiographical poem within the Arthurian cycle. Describing the establishment of a Company of Co-inherence within Taliessin's personal household, the poem articulates Williams' concept of co-inherence and the key principles upon which the concept is based. In *The Taliessin Poems of Charles Williams*, Anne Ridler states:

> The mythical figures of C. W.'s imagination were created, as we know, from the characters and places of his actual life. The Company described in the poem bears the same relation to this Order [Williams' Order of Co-inherence] as does the 'king's poet' to Charles himself, or, say, the City of God to its exemplar in Amen House [Oxford University Press headquarters].[18]

Moreover, quoting Williams from *The Figure of Arthur* in *The Arthurian Torso*,[19] Roma A. King, Jr., in *The Pattern in the Web*, points out:

> Of "The Founding of the Company," we can say what Williams said about another: 'A thousand preachers have said all that Dante says and left their hearers discontented; why does Dante content? Because an Image of profundity is there.'[20]

King further suggests:

> The poem becomes less a statement than a complex image that finds its archetype in the esoteric word *perichoresis* in line 106. Williams uses the word, however, not because it is esoteric, but because it images accurately the experience that he wishes his readers to feel. The poem is less to persuade than to captivate, less to convert than to expand horizons.[21]

The poem challenges the reader to submit to the captivity and to penetrate its farthest horizons.

Williams begins the poem by placing the theme within a historical context of the founding of monastic orders, beginning with St. Pachomius at Tabennisi in 320 A.D., the first coenobitic monastery, moving on to the Cappadocian Fathers and, lastly, St. Benedict's Monte Cassino in 529 A.D. He points out that this type of fellowship is growing in Logres. However, it is less than a monastic order. In contrast, the Company's fellowship is a loose structure simply pointing to a certain way of life. The Company begins in Taliessin's household, and Taliessin himself cannot account for its growth. What he does know is that love lies at its central core, grounded in the "Acts of the Throne,"[22] the doctrine of largesse. Furthermore, the Company is completely voluntary, and any soul may join simply by electing the Way. Its clarion call is "quicunque vult" ["whoever wants to"];[23] its creed is of the Trinity and the Incarnation; its rule, the doctrine of largesse; and its vow, the telling of the love of each for each, and of the Incarnation for all. Through the Company, auroral Logres' potentialities can be realized.

Williams moves on to the Company's internal structure. It is a three-tiered construct with the first station consisting of:

> those who lived by a frankness of honourable exchange,
> labour in the kingdom, devotion in the Church, the need
> each had of other; this was the measurement and motion
> of process—the seed of all civil polity... .[24]

The first tier, therefore, consists of the everyman's dedication to oversee the provision and execution necessary for the sustenance of the community. And upon what is this dedication constituted?

> the making of a mutual beauty in exchange,
> be the exchange dutiful or freely debonair;
> duty so and debonair freedom mingled,
> taking and giving being the living of largesse,
> and in less than this the kingdom having no saving.[25]

In the "second mode," Williams envisions an extension of the dimension of the first. While the Company's first station is predicated upon exchange and largesse, the second perceives an additional facet to Williams' world of crystalline geometry.

The Company's second mode bore farther
the labour and fruition; it exchanged the proper self
and wherever need was drew breath daily
in another's place, according to the grace of the Spirit
'dying each other's life, living each other's death.'[26]

The additional facet is substitution. The Incarnation dies willingly and without reservation in its "first creation." Thus, the cosmos is ordained in the Ways of Affirmation and Negation. This understanding was already known by the contemplatives, but now, through the Company, it is shared with all.

none of the Company—
in marriage, in the priesthood, in friendship, in all love—
forgot in their own degree the decree of substitution.[27]

As a result, the Company's second tier consists of those with knowledge of substitution, in addition to the knowledge of exchange and largesse possessed by the first station.

Few enter upon the Company's third station. It is a level that penetrates beyond the horizon to the cosmos' deepest phenomena. The third station's insight is reserved for those experiencing full salvation and Trinitarian co-inherence "restored / by the one adored substitution."[28] It can be equated with "the Flesh-taking sufficed / the God-bearer to make her a sharer in Itself."[29] Moreover, with Taliessin engaged at this level, he expresses an image in verse of Camelot's potentialities achieved:

the law willed and fulfilled and walking in Camelot…
he had seen afar
a deep, strange island of granite growth, [upon this rock I will build my Church]
thrice charged with massive light in change,
clear and golden-cream and rose tinctured,
each in turn the Holder and the Held…
beyond Carbonek, beyond Broceliande,
in the land of the Trinity, the land of the perichoresis.[30]

What is the perichoresis of which the poet speaks? It is the image's quintessence, the Trinity unveiled for humankind's spiritual enlightenment. It is:

separateness without separation, reality without rift,

where the Basis [the Father] is in the Image [the Son],
and the Image in the Gift [the Holy Spirit],
the Gift is in the Image and the Image in the Basis,
and the Basis and Gift alike in Gift and Basis.[31]

An apprehension of the perichoresis, then, gives expression to the third station's unique quality.

However, the separation of the stations is a separation in degrees of spiritual experience and understanding. It is not a separation by social, economic or political rank. In the Company, all are equal under the Incarnation and substitution of the Cross; the parity shared by all lies in the cosmos' indwelling in the heart of the Divine Mercy.

The remainder of the poem takes up Williams' theme of excellent absurdity. The setting is the rose garden. Taliessin is in a perplexed state, waiting for the voice to express what lies within his heart. As he daydreams, his perplexity is compounded by the sudden appearance before him of an image of his beloved Dindrane, "the vision of verse," or, as Williams states, the "analogical substitution," the actual face of Dinadan.

Dindrane is Taliessin's Beatrice, "a figure of sanctity and self-giving. She is what Guinevere should have been, and, upon her death, she will be taken by Galahad, Percivale and Bors with queenly homage to the land of the Trinity, Sarras, for burial."[32] On the other hand is Dinadan. He is considered "the wisest next to Galahad, Taliessin and Merlin, knowing his place [within the Company and the kingdom] and seeing himself as dispensable, while accepting humiliation with laughter."[33]

Dinadan addresses Taliessin, "Well encountered, lieutenant / (they call you) of God's new grace in the streets of Camelot."[34] Taliessin is aghast at the suggestion that he is the Company's lieutenant, fearing sinful pride in acknowledging any primary position within the movement. Dinadan gently reprimands him,

> Sir, God is the origin and the end God;...
> any buyer of souls is bought himself by his purchase;
> take the lieutenancy for the sake of the shyness the excellent absurdity holds.[35]

Taliessin replies:
'Must I be once more superfluous?

as to Dindrane and the kingdom, so to the Company,
verse is superfluous, and I even to verse.'[36]

Dinadan goes on to explain the excellent absurdity to Taliessin. He tells Taliessin that God exists in and of Himself. Therefore, all humankind and its achievements are truly superfluous to God's reality and exist only because of God's divine mercy and grace. Dinadan declares:

> The God bearer
> is the prime and sublime image of entire superfluity.
> If an image lacks, since God backs all,
> be the image, a needless image of peace
> to those in peace; to you an image of modesty.
> This purchase of modesty is nothing new;
> In the cause is your comfort, in your comfort also the cause.
> Take the largesse; think yourself the less; bless heaven.[37]

Thus, Dinadan outlines our own superfluity to the plan of the Divine Mercy. We are merely actors upon His stage and within His play. However, it behooves us to accept whatever role we are asked to play. While we can accept or reject freely, in accepting, we are consecrated in His holy grace. Moreover, by embracing the role, we acknowledge its superfluity to the entire structure of His play, and how blessed we are to be asked. This is the excellent absurdity.

The final stanza of the poem celebrates the Company and Taliessin. The king's poet is hailed as the Company's single bond. The Company itself is described as unformulated, unvowed, full of joy and laughter, far exceeding similar circumstances in the households of the great lords. But, most importantly, equality of being is ordained through all stations. The final stanza concludes:

> The Company throve by love, by increase of peace,
> by the shyness of saving and being saved in others—
> the Christ-taunting and Christ-planting maxim
> which throughout Logres the excellent absurdity held.[38]

In this, auroral Logres' central poem, Williams explores the achievement of potentialities. Taliessin creates a Company of Co-inherence reflecting the Trinity's unity and functioning as a counter to the Fall, whether of Adam or the kingdom. At its core lies a cosmic equality of being and existence within the Divine Mercy.

Exchange and substitution are the basic conditions for its growth and sustenance.

Furthermore, Williams reveals the Trinity's nature in a vision so unique it causes serious thought as to Williams' personal experience with the essence of the Trinity. In mirroring the Imagination's reflection, his poetic imagination seems fully conjoined with the Imagination. Conjecture is mere speculation; however, in this case, is the imaginative so vivid and distinctive, and is the description so sharply detailed, that abstract reasoning and judgment can lead to only one conclusion? Williams is co-inherent with the Divine. He has joined the pantheon of the saints.

Finally, there is the proposal of excellent absurdity. The concept is based upon Matthew 27, "Others he saved; himself he could not save," which is based on the presumption that Christ was incapable of saving Himself from final humiliation and subsequent death. The question is, had He chosen to do so, would not the substitution and exchange have been incomplete? Moreover, would not humankind's redemption have been incomplete? The fulfillment of the promise requires a resurrection. Without humiliation and death, there can be no Resurrection. Therefore, to save Himself is an abrogation of the most important promise ever made to humankind: the promise of a life after death in co-inherence with the Holy Trinity. This is the excellent absurdity: He could save Himself, but for the love of His creation, He freely chose not to, choosing, rather, to save others.

Auroral Logres' final poem is *The Departure of Dindrane*. It contains two intertwining threads consisting of Dindrane's departure for the convent at Almesbury to fulfill her life in the Ascetic Way, and the decision facing a slave girl, who, in her purity and sanctity, is a mirror of Dindrane. The weaving together of the two tales creates tension; for the one, a decision has already been made, while, for the other, a decision is yet to be made. Ultimately, Dindrane's decision will influence the slave girl in a manner not readily apparent at the poem's opening.

In addition, there is Taliessin, Dindrane's platonic lover, the archetypical unicorn incapable of physical consummation due to the indivisible passion for his art and his purpose, and now facing his own challenge. He freely surrenders to Dindrane's decision, though the pain felt is his Calvary's spear, yet surrender he does, because in surrender is greater love than in rivalry. Commenting on this point, C. S. Lewis states:

There may have been conflict in the soul of each at some earlier state; we are not shown that stage. In each of them now the natural passion is not so much 'mortified,' as set on fire, by the spiritual: their human love survives in their fully and rapturously accepted vocations as red-hot coal survives in fire; nay, it is now vocation as the red coal *is* the fire.[39]

The first stanza establishes the physical setting for the journey's commencement. The key element is the condition of rain, setting an atmosphere not of gloom so much as a state of grayness similar to the background sky of a watercolor's rainy landscape. The Company gathers to escort Dindrane to the convent at Almesbury.

The second stanza is contrapuntal to Dindrane's anticipated departure, a decision already made. Its theme is the slave girl's pending decision concerning her future. In regard to that decision, the old Levitical law regarding slavery is explained. At the end of seven years, a slave is offered the option of freedom. There are actually three possibilities at this stage: to be sent to a former land with a purse of coins; to receive, if a woman, a dowry, or "for a man a farm / or a place in a guild or the army;"[40] or, to freely return to the household of former irrevocable servitude.

The next stanza establishes the poem's tension. The slave girl, through whose eyes the whole poem is envisioned, faces the decision described above.

> Now near freedom, she brooded on the choice—
> this her last errand, but where to cast
> her future in seven days' time eluded purpose:... .[41]

The scene delineates her dilemma, as, confronting her choices, she considers all three, especially the third, for she has been happy in Taliessin's household.

> [O]r to swear herself still of the household, and leave
> what end would to come—and then to grieve
> perchance for all forgone;...[42]

The choice is serious, the consequences uncertain as the tension mounts. At this precise moment, Dindrane emerges into the day's grayness, accompanied by Elayne, Bor's wife, and Taliessin, the king's poet. They are her two best friends, and they have "brought her that day / to the court of separation, affirmation into rejection."[43] Dindrane is rejecting the Way of Affirmation and, with affirmation, is accepting the Way of Rejection. She has freely chosen separation from those she loves as she seeks unity with the Greater Love.

The following stanza is entirely from the slave girl's perspective. She surmises the pain her lord is feeling, in contrast to the "chrism of dedication / shining already" upon Dindrane's brow; Taliessin's "schism," Dindrane's "chrism."

> She measured herself against her [Dindrane], in a suddenly now
> new-treasured servitude; she saw there
> love and a live heart in Dindrane
> and all circumstance of bondage blessed in her body
> moving to a bondage—to a new panoplied category.[44]

She experiences a new awareness. Can servitude be so bad? Dindrane's heart is open to her purpose, "Love and a live heart lay in Dindrane; / love and a live heart sprang in the slave."[45] The girl's intellect perceives directly what Taliessin and Dindrane have already incorporated into the forefront of their combined consciousness, "servitude and freedom were one and interchangeable."[46]

Subsequently, Williams defines both servitude and freedom in the following stanza's opening lines: "Servitude is a will that obeys an imaged law; / freedom is unimaged—or makes choice of images."[47] The imaged law is the equivalent of "neither is this Thou," while the unimaged equates to "this also is Thou." In *Essential Writings in Spirituality and Theology*, Charles Hefling states:

> Neither of these ways is entirely independent of the other, and their watchwords are the two halves of one saying, which Williams treats as a quotation although he never found its source: this also is Thou; neither is this Thou. 'As a maxim for living,' he said of this formula, 'it is invaluable, and it—or its reversal—summarizes the history of the Christian Church.'[48]

Moreover, contrary to Hefling's conclusion that Williams never found the source of the quote: the quotation originates with one of the esteemed Church Fathers, St. Ephrem the Syrian, commenting on how the more a person comes to contemplate God in nature, the more that person realizes that God is also above and beyond nature.[49]

Further, the quotation is Williams' literary expression for articulating the apprehension of transcendence through the Way of Affirmation of images and the Way of Rejection of images. Consequently, Williams describes Taliessin and Dindrane's journey as follows:

> Ways upon the Way…
> cloaked in the dim day, on the highroad of the hazel [symbolizing straightness, and discipline][50]
> between city and convent, the two great vocations,
> the Rejection of all images before the unimaged,
> the Affirmation of all images before the all-imaged,
> the Rejection affirming, the Affirmation rejecting, the king's poet riding through a cloud [of unknowing] with an avowed novice,
> and either no less than the other the doctrine of largesse;[51]

This is complementary spirituality, leading to the same end while simultaneously uniting both Taliessin and Dindrane, the affirmer and the negator, an outcome Williams projects for the Company, the community and the kingdom.

What choice will the slave girl make, or is the decision already reached, the choice inevitable in light of all she is witnessing? At this juncture, the girl hears a voice from the third heaven, the region of the summer stars, earth's cone's point of shadow, and, once more Williams expresses, as only he can, the ephemeral nature of time's relevance within a spiritual pattern. The yet unborn Galahad speaks to her:

> It was toned to sweetness of note disowned by the world
> while the world was self-owned…
> the future comes to pass in a fleeting light,
> the foster-ward of Dindrane before his birth:
> 'Fair lord, salute me to my lord Sir Lancelot my father,
> and bid him remember of this unstable world.'
> The grand Rejection sang to the grand Affirmation;
> itself affirming, itself honouring, its peer:
> 'Salute me, salute me, to my lord Sir Lancelot my father.'[52]

Roma A. King, Jr. maintains that the voice is "an encouragement to affirm all things in this unstable world as images of the All-imaged."[53] Without Dindrane's choice of Almesbury and all it portends at this precise moment on time's continuum, is Galahad's future achievement attainable?

The moment of parting for Taliessin and Dindrane is at hand. The slave girl bears witness to the burning passion that mortification stokes. The complementary ways are separate, yet united in their spirituality and conclusion, and, cementing this point, the following exchange takes place:

> He said: 'Blessed one, what shall I wish you now
> but a safe passage through all the impersonalities [negations and denials]?'
> And she: 'Most blessed lord, what shall I wish
> but the return of the personalities [affirmations and acceptances], beyond
> the bond and blessing of departure of personality?
> I will affirm, my beloved, all that I should.'
> And he: 'I will reject all that I should—
> yes, and affirm; the term of Camelot, my adored,
> lies at the term of Almesbury.[54]

In the brief concluding stanza, the slave girl chooses servitude in Taliessin's household. She realizes that in negation is affirmation and in affirmation, negation. She understands the complementary spirituality. "For the slave and the princess, the worker and the contemplative, are co-inherent and neither can be fully understood without the other."[55]

The final line of the poem demonstrates the slave girl's pure apprehension of transcendent truth. "They only can do it with my lord who can do it without him, / and I know he will have about him only those."[56] What is the transcendent truth she meditates on? C. S. Lewis explains, "The Father can be well pleased in that Son only who adheres to the Father when apparently forsaken. The fullest grace can be received by those only who continue to obey during the dryness in which all grace seems to be withheld. The same is true, in degree, of every human master."[57]

In conclusion, Williams reveals the possibilities of brilliant splendor within Logres' grasp as he explores love's potentialities. For, within love's potentialities, Logres can achieve the greatness for which it is destined as the womb for the Second Coming. There is the realization that love and the Divine are one and inseparable, and it can be articulated in comparative and contrasting configurations. There is the Divine's love for the Divine in the abstraction of the Holy Trinity. Likewise, the Incarnation confirms the Divine's love for humanity. In contrast, humankind's love for the Divine is conditional upon the free choice bestowed in the Garden of Opportunity, and humanity's love for humanity lies in the multiple possibilities of companionship, community and kingdom.

Paradoxically, there is also the excellent absurdity that the Divine does not need humanity's love to fulfill Its potentiality. However, humankind needs the Divine's love to fulfill its mission, within creation's design, to enter into the grace of the Trinity and the Incarnation. Above all else, in Williams' view, love's greatest potential is the capacity to overcome all barriers of time and space, allowing humankind to enter into the realm of infinity and extending humanity's fingertip to the fingertip of the Divine.

---

[1] *Holy Bible*. 1 Cor. 9:27.
[2] Williams, "Answers" 3.
[3] Williams and Lewis, *Taliessin*, "Taliessin's Song of the Unicorn" L21-25.
[4] Ibid. L29-36.
[5] Ridler 30.
[6] Williams and Lewis, *Taliessin*, "Bors to Elayne: The Fish of Broceliande" L9.
[7] Ibid. L25.
[8] Ibid. L30.
[9] King 56.
[10] Ridler 32.
[11] Williams and Lewis, *Taliessin*, "Taliessin on the Death of Virgil" L9-13.
[12] Ibid. L15-18.
[13] Ibid. L19-25.
[14] Williams and Lewis 305.
[15] Williams and Lewis, *Taliessin*, "Virgil" L30.
[16] Ibid. L39-41.
[17] Williams, "Answers" 4.
[18] Ridler 95.
[19] Williams and Lewis 212.
[20] King 151.
[21] Ibid.
[22] Williams and Lewis, *Summer*, "Founding" L13.
[23] Ibid. L23.
[24] Ibid. L43-46.
[25] Ibid. L55-59.
[26] Ibid. L60-64.
[27] Ibid. L74-76.

28 Ibid. L86-87.
29 Ibid. L89-90.
30 Ibid. L96-106.
31 Ibid. L107-110.
32 Spaeth 2.
33 Ibid.
34 Williams and Lewis, *Summer*, "Founding" L121-122.
35 Ibid. L127-132.
36 Ibid. L133-135.
37 Ibid. L144-153.
38 Ibid. L162-165.
39 Williams and Lewis 336.
40 Williams and Lewis, *Summer*, "The Departure" L18-19.
41 Ibid. L25-27.
42 Ibid. L31-33.
43 Ibid. L45-46.
44 Ibid. L56-60.
45 Ibid. L71-72.
46 Ibid. L77.
47 Ibid. L78-79.
48 Hefling 15.
49 Schakel, Letter 14, para. 6.
50 Spaeth 6.
51 Williams and Lewis, *Summer*, "Departure" L84-91.
52 Ibid. L125-136.
53 King 150.
54 Williams and Lewis, *Summer*, "Departure" L152-155.
55 Williams and Lewis 336.
56 Williams and Lewis, *Summer*, "Departure" L172-173.
57 Williams and Lewis 338-339.

Chapter 6

The Uncoupling of Empire: Seeds of Destruction

The main theme of the poems comprising this section is an investigation of the seeds of destruction planted in Logres by the same serpentine presence as in the Garden of Opportunity. The essential issue, destruction, has already been anticipated in Williams' epigraph to *Taliessin through Logres* when he quotes from Dante's *De Monarchia*, I, iii:

> Unde est, quod non operatio propria propter essentiam, sed haec propter illam habet ut sit.
>
> Hence it is that the proper operation does not exist for the sake of the essence, but the essence has its being for the sake of the operation.[1]

With this quotation, Williams is also suggesting the metaphorical aspect of his Arthuriad, reflecting the cosmic movement of humankind from creation to the inevitable and ultimate consciousness of the Divine. Furthermore, if we see *The Empire Ascendant* as an expression of the potential of the Creator's creation and *Auroral Logres* as representative of the brilliant opportunities available in this new Garden of Opportunity, then we must see *The Uncoupling of Empire*, with the planting of seeds of destruction, as serpentine temptations assumed, resulting in humankind's corruption and the kingdom's relegation to a base status within creation and the cosmic order.

Creation is the Divine's first gift to His children. The Divine's children are placed in it through the exchange of the Father with His creation. The children's purpose is to serve the Creator through the creation. However, because, through the wiles of the serpent, the children come to desire equality with the Godhead, their craving is frustrated by a degree of knowledge they cannot anticipate as resulting in humankind's fall from grace. Because the Fall insures a complete misunderstanding of humankind's function and purpose within the universal design, the children come to know evil, not as imperfection of God's creation, nor as revolt against the Godhead, but, rather, as the misdirection of their own creation, thus offending the exchange which resulted in their existence. Consequently, since the Fall, the cosmic purpose of humankind is to realign once again with the proper function of humankind's creation and to serve the Creator through his creation.

This chapter explores the impediments to the fulfillment of Logres' potential. All the evils and threats of evil already exist in the kingdom. Humankind's free will can choose to overcome the evils or succumb to them. However, to succumb is to foil the Grail's mission to actualize the Matter of Britain to be witness to the Parousia and experience the fruition of the perichoresis.

The Crowning of Arthur is specifically assigned to this section; within the poem, Williams treats the root of all the failures in Logres and the very makeup of Arthur's character. However, prior to examining that character, it is important to examine the celebratory environment in which the king's fatal flaw is revealed.

Externally, all appears well as, at the stroke of midnight, the king is crowned amid the splendor and reflection of almost Pentecostal fires. There is jubilation highlighted by the flaunting flags of the king's lords. Above all is stationed the king's dragon flag. Next is Lancelot's lion flag. It is Lancelot who, unknowingly, is to execute the strategy for governance already determined within Arthur's brain.

Merlin is also in attendance. He is the architect of all that is occurring, for he lies behind Arthur's rise to this moment of glory. Yet, during the celebration, Merlin chooses to climb the many steps to the top of the dome of St. Stephen, mythical Camelot's mythical church,[2] a church dedicated to a saint who has "looked up to heaven and [seen] the glory of God, and Jesus standing at the right hand of God. 'Look,' he said, 'I see heaven open and the Son of Man standing at the right hand of God.'"[3]

As Merlin peers from the dome, he sees off in the distance the dome of Sophia. However, St. Sophia, the church of the Emperor [God], devoted to Divine Wisdom, is real and the center of Christian belief in the Byzantine Empire. In Merlin's imagination, however, the mythical St. Stephen and the tangible St. Sophia are linked, as are the mythical Camelot and the material Byzantium. In *The Crowning*, Williams states: "he looked through the depth to the dome of Sophia; / the kingdom and the power and the glory chimed."[4] The Empire is co-inherent.

What follows is a description of the festivities' heraldic glory interspersed with observations by the presage, Merlin, and the court poet, Taliessin. The reflecting torchlight reveals the glory of Percivale's glowing star-pointed banner, as well as Queen Morgause leaning from a casement window, already bearing the source of Arthur's bane begotten through an incestuous encounter with her half-brother, Arthur. The impassioned flames reflect in shadows on her brow, and around her neck she wears Lord Lamorack's sable. Next is the banner of Dinadan portraying a swimming dolphin on the primary field. The playful dolphin mirrors the pliant personality of its master, the delight of Dinadan in life, and his appreciation of the excellent absurdity within his vision's range. The final major banner replicates Bors' symbol of charity, the pelican, the Christian image of the Cross and the Crucifixion.

Once again, Merlin views the scene before him and considers the numerous beasts and fish upon the banners of the participants. He cannot help but meditate on his mother, Nimue, "the great mother and lady of Broceliande—Nature, as it were, or all the vast processes of the universe imaged in a single figure."[5] She represents the glory of Logres, hierarchic and republican, the "patterns of the Logos."[6]

In contrast to Merlin's objective view, Taliessin's view is subjectively articulated from a position within the crowd. He, too, sees the many representations of nature upon the lords' banners. However, to him they are systematic and organized archetypes of mathematics' symmetry. The "star and moon, dolphin and pelican, lion and leopard" mirror the cosmos' symmetrical interconnection and the Divine Mercy's co-inherent universe.

The sound of flutes suddenly overwhelms the noise of the crowd. Gawaine's thistle banner and Bedivere's rose draw near. The young queen Guinevere's chalice banner follows; the chalice, on a red background within a white field, is symbolic of Guinevere's predestined role as mother to Logres' future. Lancelot escorts the queen, and Williams describes him as follows:

> the king's organic motion, the king's mind's blood,
> the lion in the blood roaring through the mouth of creation
> as the lions roar that stand in the Byzantine glory.[7]

Williams' Lancelot is so close to the king as to be his alter ego. He is an organic representative of the king's mind and the very blood flowing through the king's brain. This right hand of Arthur's is a lion roaring through the king's veins at this very moment of the kingdom's creation, functioning like the stone lion guardians at Byzantium's throne room entrance and biblically reminiscent of the approving lions at Solomon's judgmental proclamations.

In the very next stanza, the most grievous seed of Logres' destruction is sown, for, as the king gazes upon the city, he entertains the root evil that consumed Adam. Williams writes:

> the king for the kingdom, or the kingdom made for the king?
> Thwart drove his current against the current of Merlin:
> in beleaguered Sophia they sang of the dolorous blow.[8]

As he mulls thoughts of equality with the Godhead, Arthur is guilty of Adam's sin. Pride's attitude is contrary to Merlin's vision of a heaven-centered kingdom, ministered by a loyal servant of the Eternal. In beleaguered Sophia, defending itself against the Muslim invaders, there is conscious awareness of the dolorous blow that has been struck against the kingdom's purpose. The king chooses not to serve the Creator through His creation; rather he chooses to have the Creator's creation serve him. Mihal states, "A key issue for C. W. in his radical re-interpretation of the Arthurian legend is the king's fatal/fateful misunderstanding of his own function/purpose. Arthur's error [pride] becomes the root of all the failures in Logres. Recall C. W.'s epigraph."[9]

This single thought of Arthur is also a dolorous blow, because he intends to use the kingdom for his own purpose. Williams observes:

> It is this turning point of the most sacred of mysteries to the immediate security of the self that is the catastrophic thing... [Through this act of pride] Man wounds himself. It is an image of the Fall; it is also an image of every individual and deliberate

act of malice, though the deliberation is here but passionate and not coldly angry.[10]

The King's fatal flaw marks the beginning of the end for the kingdom. The Matter of Britain is no longer sustainable.

In the final two stanzas, Taliessin sees the kingdom consumed on a pyre. And, at the fire's peak, the figures of Arthur and Lancelot, represented by lion and dragon, embrace in a dance of death, clawing, twisting and screaming. Warring, they devour each other, the king unto his tomb, and the knight unto his destiny, doomed except for his son's existence. The effects radiate throughout the Empire:

> the spark of Logres fades, glows, fades.
> It is the first watch; the Pope says Matins in Lateran;
> the hollow call is beaten on the board in Sophia;
> the ledge of souls shudders, whether they die or live.[11]

Roma A. King, Jr. places the conclusion of the poem in perspective when he states, "Thus the poem that began with a glory of light and celebration ends with shuddering souls awaiting the judgment that shall decree whether they live or die. The answer for Logres, however, is suspended for the time being. The end awaits the passage of time."[12]

Critics generally agree that no poem within the *Uncoupling* cycle generates more illustrations of Arthur's kingdom's core decay than *Lamorack and the Queen Morgause of Orkney*. For example, C. S. Lewis states, "[this poem] draws together into one vision all the evils and threats of evil that there are in Logres."[13] Anne Ridler, in *The Taliessin Poems of Charles Williams*, points out that *Lamorack* is "a poem of terrible fate with no hint of salvation."[14] Roma A. King, Jr. declares, "[the poem creates] a tension between passivity and movement, and the ponderous but inexorable progress of the action toward its dreaded end."[15] Lewis further articulates that:

> C. W.'s concern [in this poem] is not with the psychological origins of evil, but with its metaphysical 'procession,' its intrusion from nightmare into reality, the horrible stages whereby what ought to be not at all becomes an image, and what ought to be only an image becomes stone, and what ought to be stone becomes a woman, and what ought to be only a woman becomes her son... Williams' myth of the Fall portrays evil as miscreation—the bringing to be of what must not be, yet now it is.[16]

The poem consists of three sections. Stanzas one through three depict Lamorack's first impressions upon seeing Queen Morgause, Lot's wife. Lot is Orkney's king, ruler of windswept islands in the North Atlantic off the coast of northeast Scotland. Lamorack views Morgause as hued stone bruising his bone and entering his eye in an aberrant expression. Unknown to Lamorack, this first impression is an image of Morgause's evil. Her face resembles a pre-Adamic sculpture which has been "torn from its rock [and] was swept away."[17] However, once the stone is torn from its mooring and swept away, the queen becomes part of what must follow within Arthur's kingdom, for she plays an integral part in the fall of Arthur and his kingdom. Moreover, Morgause is a rigid tornado, a paradoxical fusing of stone and storm, of hardness and mobility contrasted with motion and activity. The existence of this inanimate and subhuman creature can only result in schism for the kingdom and creation.

In his characteristic juxtaposing of events, Williams next explains why Lamorack comes to be in the Orkney Islands to begin with. He is on a mission from the king to explore Lot's kingdom's coast. What follows are impressions of the land he surveys: a roaring sea on the one hand, caves and hollows filled with screaming gulls on the other. He hears their harsh cries and sees hideous huge figures hewn by the winds and the sea. Lamorack remembers the archbishop in Caerleon preaching:

> that before the making of man or beast
> the Emperor knew all carved contingent shapes
> in torrid marsh temples or on cold crookt capes.
> These were the shapes only the Emperor knew.[18]

The key phrase is "contingent shapes" known only by the Emperor that represent what might be, but need not be. This is the knowledge of evil in the Godhead's mind. However, in humankind's prideful attempt to seek equality with the Universe's knowledge, the contingent becomes an actuality to humanity. Williams portrays the evil observed through Lamorack's eyes:

> Ship and sculpture shuddered: the crag's scream
> mingled with the seamews'; Logres' convulsed theme
>   [action and meaning]
> wailed in the whirlwind; we fled before the storms,
> and behind us loosed in the air flew giant inhuman forms.[19]

Unaware, Lamorack is witnessing the seismic convulsion present at the Fall and humankind's flight from the Garden of Eden before giant non-human forms, Michael's soldier angels. This is Orkney's environment, which also nurtures the anomalistic Morgause, who is a significant source of another's fall.

The next stanza begins the third and concluding section of the poem. Lamorack returns from his mission and is present in the great, grim hall of King Arthur. There sits the king between two queens, Guinevere on his right and Morgause on his fateful left. The eyes of Morgause remind Lamorack of the sculptured shapes of the cliffs he has recently seen. Moreover, around her stand her four sons, Lot's offspring. A fifth, incest's son with Arthur, is present if not in view. As Morgause stirs, Lamorack hears once again the seamews' screams "in the envy of the unborn bastard."[20] For Modred's conception is an offense against the law of exchange temporarily foiling the Grail's work.

Merlin now reveals to Lamorack the meaning of what his mind's eye is witnessing. Morgause's face is a reflection of Arthur's, so each will darken the other's. But Merlin's question is, "How can this be?"

After he participates in carnal knowledge with his sister, Arthur's fate is split, resulting in the contingent knowledge of evil actualized again, as it was once before in the Garden of Opportunity. Modred's incestuous conception is a major source of the kingdom's fall, but Galahad's mystical conception is redemption's wellspring and embodies humankind's capacity for the Divine, offering hope through possibility.

Despite Merlin's revelations to Lamorack, the latter's fate is chosen with his own free will. In his subconscious, he sees the child, Modred, lying

> unborn in the queen's womb;
> unformed in his brain is the web of all our doom,
> as unformed in the minds of all the great lords
> lies the image of the split Table and of surreptitious swords.
> [Yet] I am the queen's servant: while I live.[21]

In his essay, "Notes on the Arthurian Myth," Williams states:

> The fatality, the curse [which is the ban against the coming of the Grail], the result of the Dolorous Blow, has to work itself out through the King. He and his two sisters—Morgause and

Morgan—are man loving himself and hating himself. This—and not mere incest—is the reason that Modred is born of Arthur and Morgause, and Modred is entire egotism, Arthur's self-attention carried to the final degree [the kingdom for the king].[22]

Lamorack and the Queen Morgause of Orkney expresses three key elements in the kingdom's collapse. First, there is Lamorack's obsession with Morgause. Lewis suggests, "The heavy fetters of an obsession may prove even more lasting than the "golden snare' of Euclidean, poetic and intellectual love. This is Lamorack's personal tragedy: with it are mixed two tragedies darker still."[23] The darker tragedies are Arthur's incest, while intending only fornication, resulting in Modred, betrayer and killer of Arthur.

Second, there is the contingent knowledge of evil descended upon humankind at humankind's own invitation. Lewis again:

> And all these things are so because Man is fallen. The lust and fierceness of Morgause, the lust and weakness of Arthur... the future treachery of Modred, are all specimens of those 'contingent' things which God knew but would not create and which the foolish Adam insisted upon experiencing... Seeing them, he [Adam] knows at once they are things which only the Emperor [God] should have known.[24]

Third, there is the vision of a Fall—but whose? Mihal states, "Merlin reveals to Lamorack that his [Lamorack's] vision of Morgause and Arthur together is a vision of the original Fall, but this time it is Camelot's."[25] "Over Camelot and Carbonek a whirling creature hovered / as over the Adam in Eden when they found themselves uncovered."[26] Finally, Williams' metaphysical procession is complete. The nightmare is now reality. The second Fall is done.

Bors to Elayne: on the King's Coins is a continuation of *The Fish of Broceliande*. While *Broceliande* deals with romantic love, based upon the exchange between a man and a woman, *the King's Coins* carries the concept of exchange into the complex arena of social order. Here, Bors, the everyman, soldier, husband, lord of a self-sustaining estate and participant in incarnational exchange on a conscious and personal level, practices the process within the fabric of the Way of Affirmation.

The poem consists of two sections. The first is an expression of exchange's perfection in stanzas one and two, the first thirty-two lines of the poem. Williams forms a frame of reference against which material economy can be contrasted. Exchange's perfection is established in the following lines:

> at the turn of the day, and none only to earn;
> in the day of the turn, and none only to pay;
> for the hall is raised to the power of exchange of all
> by the small spread organisms of your hands; O Fair,
> there are the altars of Christ the City extended.[27]

Here is an expression of perfect exchange. In Bors' world, laborers, from lord and lady to worker and mechanic, earn and pay for their daily bread through daily inclined effort. Jay A. Mihal suggests, "[the key ingredient] is essential sharing in the 'power of exchange'… No one is taking advantage of anyone else because everyone understands that they are in it together."[28] King goes further when he states, "the hall becomes a prototype of the City and Elayne's hands a paradigm of the altars of Christ, the City from which bread, physical and spiritual, is dispensed to everyone."[29]

The second portion of the poem consists of three views on the new monetary system that the king and his counselor Kay are establishing for the kingdom. They are taking incarnational exchange's transcendent realities and replacing them with secular limits. Bors is the first to question the new system.

He has a dream about the consequences of the use of coin as a medium of exchange. His fear is that "this was the true end of our making; / mother of children, redeem the new law."[30] In contrast, the king's counselor declares, "Money is the medium of exchange."[31]

Because Taliessin's view is a poet's, his concern centers upon coins as symbol. One can almost hear the dismay in his voice as he says:

> We had a good thought.
> Sir, if you made verse you would doubt symbols.
> When the means are autonomous, they are deadly; when words escape from verse they hurry to rape souls;…
> We have taught our images to be free; are we glad?
> are we glad to have brought convenient heresy to Logres?[32]

Taliessin, the court poet, knows symbols, which can act unilaterally. Once a metaphor dislodges from the poem or philosophy to which it belongs, it can only create dissension through unorthodoxy, blasphemy and idolatry, just as Adam's displacement from Eden created discord within creation's design through deceit, pride and willfulness. Therefore, the dislodged metaphor and its consequences are symbolic of the Fall of humankind. King supports Taliessin's view when he states, "symbols are only symbols, coins only coins, carriers of values and not values themselves… Autonomous coins, released archetypes, loosed figures, represent the division of the indivisible, a de-incarnation of spirit from matter."[33]

The Archbishop next expresses his view of the new medium of exchange. He addresses the issue within the framework of church doctrine:

> the everlasting house the soul discovers
> is always another's; we must lose our own ends;
> we must always live in the habitation of our lovers,
> my friend's shelter for me, mine for him.[34]

and

> what is the City's breath?—
> *dying each other's life, living each other's death.* [poet's emphasis]
> Money is a medium of exchange.[35]

The point is that money is a medium of exchange; it is not the medium of exchange recognized by church doctrine. Money is just that: only money.

We now confront the key question with which the poem deals. King places the question in context: "[Can] the law of exchange that rules the relation of families and friends be made effective in the larger social unit?"[36] If one accepts that both are inextricably woven into the same fabric that is humanity, then, King asserts, "It was to preserve the law and to restore the orderly co-inherence that Jesus gave his life in exchange for man's."[37] Furthermore, in the essay "The Cross," Williams proclaims:

> By that central substitution, which was the thing added by the Cross to the Incarnation, He became everywhere the centre of, and everywhere He energized and reaffirmed, all our substitutions and exchanges. He took what remained, after the Fall, of the torn web of humanity in all times and in all places, and not so much by a miracle of healing as by a growth within it made it whole.[38]

At the conclusion of the poem, Bors makes a final observation. The new economy, based upon a system of coinage, is replacing compact with contract. Now formal agreements between parties are based on law. Prior to the new economy, humankind's exchanges were executed within a compact or covenant, a covenant being a pledge or solemn promise. Theologically, it is the promise of God to bless those who obey Him or fulfill some other condition.

Moreover, the new economy misunderstands the purpose and spiritual reality of what it is replacing. The word "economy" comes from the Greek "oikos," meaning house and "nemein," to manage. Within a theological pattern, economy, then, can be explained as the divine plan of creation and redemption, and any specific method or era of divine government. Thus, the new economy can only be another seed for the destruction of the kingdom, for it is replacing a spiritual paradigm with a material one. The exchange it fosters is driven by monetary considerations. God is replaced. C. S. Lewis declares:

> The king's head on the coins is a death's head unless the economic life is ruled by the spirit which rules Elayne. More generally still, every Logres whereof history holds records, can only retain a 'fallacy of rational virtue' and generate Modreds in its dark womb unless the Grail comes to it. Therefore, in the meantime,
> Pray, mother of children, pray for the coins,
> pray for Camelot, pray for the king, pray.[39]

The last poem in this chapter is *Taliessin in the Rose Garden*, which focuses on Guinevere. By way of comparison, if Arthur represents a flawed character, misunderstanding his role as the kingdom's king; if Morgause serves as an image of humankind's fallen state, convulsed in a condition of anarchy out of which will issue Modred, the embodiment of Arthur's extreme flaw; and finally, if the king's coins symbolize the kingdom's degeneration from a spiritual pattern to a material one; then Guinevere must epitomize what might have been, but now can never be.

With her character as a point of reference, Williams' *Rose Garden* is at once a meditation on the feminine's divinity, a reflection on the levels of potential unity represented by womanhood and, as Mihal suggests, "a zodiacal rhapsody":

> Taliessin then recalls a vision of the Empire once vouchsafed him. In a zodiacal rhapsody, he thinks of the great 'themes and

the houses' that formed the vision. He sees in Guinevere the embodiment of one of those themes. She is an especially beautiful incarnation of the 'unity' of body and soul that has so scandalized the Greeks and the Jews.[40]

Thus, Guinevere is the feminine incarnation of humanity's unity with the Divine. This is Guinevere's potential.

The opening stanza is set in the queen's rose garden. Among the cabbage roses, each individually consisting of one hundred co-inhered petals, Taliessin works on his verse, ever the Druid-born and Byzantium-trained poet. As he looks up, he sees "three implicit figures," a vision of the Holy Trinity's feminine facet. They are:

> the feminine headship of Logres, the queen Guinevere,
> talking to Dindrane, Percivale's sister; beyond,
> as the ground-work she was and tended, a single maid
> hardened with toil on the well-gardened roses;
> what was even Dindrane but an eidolon of the slaves?[41]

This is Williams' image of the natural capacity for co-inherent unity within Logres' divine femininity.

The following stanza's focus is upon the magical ruby ring worn by Logres' consort. Williams points out:

> There, in the single central ruby [symbol of the Divine Rose's blood upon the crucifix], Taliessin saw, in the sovereign gem of Logres, the contained life of Logres-in-the-Empire.[42]

This contained life consists of a secular war expanding throughout the land and an invasion by pirates from the north who will pillage, plunder and murder the kingdom's inhabitants. The ring is so richly imbued with Merlin's magical charm that Taliessin can also see the encased roses' color melting into King Pelles' blood, a result of the Dolorous Blow. Taliessin's reaction to this vision: "The Wounded Rose runs with the blood of Carbonek."[43] Pelles' wound is thus compared to the "Wounded Rose," which is an image for the crucified Christ. C. S. Lewis suggests that "in the ruby stone Taliessin is seeing both the Fall and the Redemption."[44] The Fall is depicted as the envisioned civil wars and chaotic invasions and the Redemption by the blood of Christ's vicar at Carbonek, Pelles.

The following stanza refocuses upon the person of Guinevere. Taliessin sees how the queen searches the shadows of the garden for

Lancelot. He recalls the story of Tristam and King Mark, both in love with Queen Iseult, and just as Palomides studied the poetic Iseult, Taliessin studies and searches for "the zodiac in the flesh," the true significance of woman, in Guinevere. The tragedy lies in Guinevere's inability to reflect the image of woman that Taliessin seeks. He states, "bitter is the brew of exchange," especially when "the beauty made is not the beauty meant," and reviled "is pride [the Fall's sin] while the Rose-King bleeds at Carbonek."[45]

Stanza four is the longest in the poem. In it, Taliessin will explore his zodiacal vision in precise detail through the myth of the Zodiac. Thelma Shuttleworth explains:

> Taliessin finds the contemporary myth of Zodiac a convenient image of the Co-inherence of the Universe. The sun makes an annual journey around the earth and the other planets (as the blood circulates through veins, arteries, organs of the human body) passing in seasonal order through the Houses (lunar months), the qualities of which are supposed, in Astrology, to influence the affairs of human beings born under their signs. The myth gives scope for contingent disasters inherent in the vagaries of natural phenomena in the universe and in mankind, and points the indissoluble relationship of each to all.[46]

Moreover, using this stanza as an introduction, Williams employs the remaining stanzas to explore woman's cosmic significance. Through Taliessin's vision, Williams investigates the cohesive capability inherent in woman's nature to coalesce even further the universe's co-inherent association among all its varied realities. In a flash of insight Taliessin explains:

> I saw how the City [the Divine Order of the Universe]
> was based, faced fair to the Emperor as the queen to the king
> slaves to lords, and all Caucasia to Carbonek.[47]

According to King, "In Byzantium Taliessin saw how the city, the bride, was faced toward the emperor, the one waiting to receive and the other to give the impregnating seed of life. They are symbolic of the interrelation of all orders of creation, queen to king, slave to lord, Caucasia to Carbonek."[48]

Thus, co-inherence's most compelling experience exists within exchange's beatific exaltation.

Furthermore, Taliessin's zodiacal vision is a continuing investigation into the co-inherent experience. Williams' imagery illustrates the indivisibility of the co-inherent relationship of all the dimensions of the universe. Taliessin sees the twelve houses of the mysterious zodiac issuing from the Throne. The Emperor's sun proceeds among them; and the seven "spiritual" planets contribute "their qualities of cause and permanence."

> [I]n each the generation of creation, in each the consummation.
> All coalesced in each; that each mind
> in the Empire might find its own kind of entry.[49]

Taliessin's point of entry is Aquarius. Through Aquarius' eyes he sees below "the rosed femininity both particled and articled, that portion withdrawn from creation's whole and the more complete portion which is creation's natural law of co-inherence. The poet asks if even Guinevere, fully articled in Camelot, can be seen other than particled within the larger Empire. The answer is no, as only her hands are seen within Gemini's Rome, the Scorpion's Jerusalem holds the privy place, while Libra's Caucasia is the base for the Earth and the queen's body. Thus the articled queen is seen in all her glory only in Logres. However, Taliessin prays that his queen may be seen "as Caucasia to Carbonek, as Logres to Sarras."[50] May she be seen as the Flesh to the Spirit, as Mankind to the Land of the Holy Trinity.

The following stanza opens with Taliessin stating, "Within and without the way wove about the image, / about the City and the body."[51] Williams is referring to several important factors. First, "the way" suggests the affirmation or rejection of images, the Romantic Way or the Ascetic Way, this also is Thou or neither is this Thou, with no image, Way or Thou exclusive of the other, but each in complementary co-inherence with the other. Second, he is advancing an image of Taliessin ascending the Sephirotic Tree, symbolic of the step-by-step process illuminating the Divine's plan as it unfolds in Creation, with a superimposed human form, the body of the City's Divine Order. Williams sees one last opportunity for Guinevere's femininity to fulfill its divine destiny as an expression for unity.

> the rays from the golden-growthed, golden-clothed arms,
> golden-sheathed and golden-breathed, imperially
> shining from above toward instruments and events,

rays shaken out towards the queen's hand stretched
to welcome the king's friend.⁵²

Thus the Throne extends the rays of opportunity to the hands that are outstretched to the king's friend, Taliessin. Moreover, Taliessin states:

> I studied universal justice
> between man and man, and (O opposite!) between man and woman
> by their own skill and the will of the Throne; light
> compact in each fitting act of justice in the City,
> and support-in-the-flesh of the sitting body of beauty
> ... let the hazel
> of verse measure the multifold levels of unity.⁵³

King points out:

> The subject here is human justice, between 'man and man, and (O opposite!) between man and woman,' but particularly the latter. Justice in their relations lies precisely in their divinely willed differences and in the reconciliation of opposites in a unity of flesh and spirit. Only "the hazel of verse,' the disciplining and shaping imagination, can suggest those 'manifold levels of unity.'⁵⁴

The question Guinevere ultimately confronts revolves around her willingness, or lack thereof, to reconcile the divinely willed differences and submit to the unity of flesh and spirit. Will Caucasia unite with Carbonek? Will the queen be the catalyst for unity? Will the queen fulfill the destiny of her divine femininity, her womanhood?

What follows is a stanza in which the hopes of Taliessin for Guinevere, Logres' feminine image, are dashed by the realities revealed to his Aquarian eyes. He witnesses the red "roseal pattern" dissolve into a pattern of "blotched blood." The zodiac churns as the Scorpion stings. "Adams blood," Cain, murders his brother while the clearness of Aquarius' eyes is diminished, engorged with blood. The Twins tear at each other, as Taliessin continues to climb the Sephoritic Tree until he reaches "the level above the magnanimous stair, and saw / the Empire dark with the incoherence of the houses."⁵⁵ Taliessin will hear the sobs of the Empire's women who share metaphysically in the Victim's sacrifice. Taliessin understands that:

> women's flesh lives the quest of the Grail
> in the charge from Camelot to Carbonek and from Carbonek to Sarras,
> puberty to Carbonek, and the stanching, and Carbonek to death.
> Blessed is she who gives herself to the journey.[56]

Blessed is the woman who freely accepts her metaphysical bond with Christ in her journey from Logres, the land of humankind, to Carbonek, the land of the Spirit, and ultimately to Sarras, the land of the Holy Trinity. Taliessin sees that Guinevere is not that woman, and so she can only contribute to the destruction of what began as a vision of Divine Glory.

In contrast, Helayne, daughter of the wounded King Pelles, is the woman who willingly accepts the Grail journey. Once again, Williams' Taliessin states:

> happy the woman who in the light of Percivale
> feels Galahad, the companion of Percivale, rise
> in her flesh, and her flesh bright in Carbonek with Christ,
> in the turn of her body, in the turn of her flesh, in the turn
> of the Heart that heals itself for the healing of others,
> when our Lord recovered the Scorpion and restored the zodiac.
> Blessed is she who can know the Dolorous Blow
> healed in the flesh of Pelles, the flesh of women;
> and hears softly with touched ears in Camelot
> Merlin magically prepare for the Rite of Galahad
> and the fixing of all fidelity from all fidelity.[57]

Here is a bold image contrasting Arthur's queen, Guinevere, and Pelles' princess, Helayne. The latter freely submits to exchange, substitution and reconciliation to restore co-inherence to a kingdom in disarray. The former wears the title of queen; however, the latter, in her selflessness, conducts herself as a queen who will partake of the Grail journey and share in the glory of Sarras.

This chapter has dealt with the seeds of the kingdom's destruction. There is Arthur's fateful pride, which places the essence of his kingship not in the service of the kingdom but, rather, the kingdom in the service of his kingship. Arthur's half-sister, Morgause, further divides the king and the kingdom from their purpose by seducing the king and giving birth to Arthur's nephew and bastard son, Modred, who will kill his father and bring the kingdom to its knees. Furthermore, Arthur will replace the kingdom's reliance for its divine individuality upon a pattern of spiritual exchange with a pattern of material exchange resulting in the loss of that special grace with which it is blessed. Finally, Guinevere, in denying her femininity's divinity and, thus, the unifying nature of womanhood, becomes the final seed in the kingdom's destruction. The Fall of the kingdom is now complete, with its knowledge of what the Emperor alone should have known.

---

[1] Williams and Lewis 18.
[2] Malory iii, 5.
[3] *Holy Bible*, Acts 7:55-56.
[4] Williams and Lewis, *Taliessin*, "Crowning" L19-20.
[5] Williams and Lewis 266.
[6] Williams and Lewis, *Taliessin*, "Crowning" L45.
[7] Ibid. L57-59.
[8] Ibid. L 63-65.
[9] Mihal 185.
[10] Williams and Lewis 269.
[11] Williams and Lewis, *Taliessin*, "Crowning" L72-75.
[12] King 48.
[13] Williams and Lewis 312.
[14] Ridler 42.
[15] King 67.
[16] Williams and Lewis 316.
[17] Williams and Lewis, *Taliessin*, "Lamorack" L8.
[18] Ibid. L22-25.
[19] Ibid. L33-36.
[20] Ibid. L44.
[21] Ibid. L73-77.
[22] Williams, "Notes" 176.
[23] Williams and Lewis 313.
[24] Ibid. 315.
[25] Mihal 212.
[26] Williams and Lewis, *Taliessin*, "Lamorack" L 53-54.
[27] Williams and Lewis, *Taliessin*, "Bors to Elayne: On the King's Coins" L24-28.
[28] Mihal 215.
[29] King 72.
[30] Williams and Lewis, *Taliessin*, "King's Coins" L52-53.
[31] Ibid. L64.
[32] Ibid. L69-74.

[33] King 74.
[34] Williams and Lewis, *Taliessin*, "King's Coins" L80-83.
[35] Ibid. L87-89.
[36] King 74.
[37] Ibid. 75.
[38] Williams, "The Cross" 137.
[39] Williams and Lewis 318.
[40] Mihal 288.
[41] Williams and Lewis, *Summer*, "Taliessin in the Rose Garden" L14-18.
[42] Ibid. L36-38.
[43] Ibid. L51.
[44] Williams and Lewis 333.
[45] Williams and Lewis, *Summer*, "Rose Garden" L65, 66-67.
[46] Ridler 89-90.
[47] Williams and Lewis, *Summer*, "Rose Garden" L76-78.
[48] King, 141.
[49] Williams and Lewis, *Summer*, "Rose Garden" L85-87.
[50] Ibid. L107.
[51] Ibid. L108-109.
[52] Ibid. L111-116.
[53] Ibid. L125-131.
[54] King 143.
[55] Williams and Lewis, *Summer*, "Rose Garden" L154-155.
[56] Ibid. L165-168.
[57] Ibid. L178-189.

Chapter 7

The Galahadian Ideal: Redemption Triumphant

This chapter examines five poems. The first two, *The Son of Lancelot* and *The Coming of Galahad*, are turning-point poems that mark a distinct departure from everything that has come before. From this point, the tone of the Arthuriad becomes more hopeful as Galahad and the Grail take center stage. They are the active forces with which Williams reveals the potential for redemption as humankind moves ever closer to its authentic cosmic significance, for humanity is meant to be the Divine's most glorious reflection within creation, a major theme of the entire Arthuriad. Moreover, humankind must never forget that only through the Incarnation of God's only Son, as a son of Adam, is this image's elegant beauty achievable. Through the Crucifixion's actualization, the Incarnation redeems humankind, forgives sin, and opens heaven's gates. This is humanity's reality and destiny, accomplished through the intervention of the Divine Mercy.

Thus far, we have moved through an examination of a symbolic second Creation with Taliessin's vision of the Empire's function as God's City on earth. Next, Williams reveals Creation's potentialities. Once again, through Taliessin, the catalytic figure in Williams' tale, we know that Logres is to have knowledge of the Grail and, as a result, become a mirror of the empire. However, due to fatal flaws within Camelot's hierarchy, humanity's pride results in a second Fall, diminishing all the potentialities of the second Creation. Who, then, is left to assume the role of a second redeemer?

For Williams, the answer is Galahad. This is not a unique conclusion, since many other writers of the Grail mythology arrived at the same conclusion. However, Williams' reason for choosing Galahad is unique. While others see Galahad as knighthood's purest ideal, Williams sees him as capable of representing much more. His interpretation is Christ-centered, making Galahad symbolic of humanity's capacity for the Divine, the Divine's most glorious reflection within Creation; while the Grail Galahad attains symbolizes humankind's Redemption through the Incarnational phenomenon of the Cross. The interaction of the Divine with the Incarnate and Galahad with the Grail drives humankind's cosmic incorporation into the Divine Infinity's pattern in a web of parallel, interlocking and simultaneously co-inherent unity.

The origin of Williams' creative interpretation is Galahad's mythical genealogy intricately entwined in the byzantine labyrinth of the Grail's history. At the foot of the Cross, Joseph of Arimathea catches Christ's blood, flowing from his side as the result of Longinus' spear thrust, with the Cup of the Last Supper. As a result, the Cup of the Last Supper, the Cup of the Cross, becomes the alchemical recipient of transmutational powers and representative of the "Second Coming." While in prison, Joseph experiences a vision in which Christ Himself makes him the first in a line of keepers of Christianity's most sacred symbols, both the Grail and the Spear. Thus, Joseph of Arimathea founds a hereditary line of Holy Hallows keepers.

King Pelles of Carbonek, located in Broceliande's forest at the crossroads between heaven, Sarras and earth, Byzantium, is a direct descendent of Joseph of Arimathea through his responsibility as keeper of the Holy Hallows. King Pelles suffers the Dolorous Blow from Longinus' spear (at Balin's hand), causing an open bleeding wound that can never heal until Pelles' descendent returns the Grail to Sarras. Alice Mary Hadfield and Anne Scott, in Ridler's *The Taliessin Poems of Charles Williams*, state:

> [The] Dolorous Blow [is] the origin of sin in the Arthurian myth.... Sir Balyn, in spite of [its] obvious sanctity, seized the spear and wounded King Pellam, who fell down, and the castle walls fell down and Sir Balyn fell down. In fact, the Fall, in an image: a holy thing used for personal gain.[1]

Thus, the ruin of Logres is placed in motion, and the analogous imagery of the Fall at Carbonek with the Fall in the Garden is illustrative, once again, of Williams' juxtaposing events out of time and space.

King Pelles' daughter, Helayne, is the Grail princess through whom the Grail keeper's hereditary genealogy continues. However, the ultimate act of exchange for the line's continuance is only possible with a worthy consort. Through the magical enchantment of Nimue, Lancelot will be lured to Carbonek. It is generally acknowledged in Arthurian mythology that Lancelot is the predetermined father of Galahad, the "Destined Knight." Once again, in his essays "Notes on the Arthurian Myths" and "Malory and the Grail Legend" Williams explains:

> Lancelot is (a) eighth in succession from Christ (8 is the number of the Christhood)... (b) the strongest and greatest knight alive... concerned with love as a thing of dolour and labour and vision.[2]
>
> He is the noblest lord in the world, the kindest, the bravest, the truest. But he will not have to do with any woman but the Queen... And Galahad must certainly be the child of the Grail-princess and certainly not of Guinevere. How is it to be consummated? It is brought about by holy enchantment and an act of substitution... He is given a cup of enchanted wine and taken to a room where the supposed Queen is: 'and all the windows and holes of that chamber were stopped that no manner of day might be seen.'[3]

King states:

> Williams finds the substitution of Helayne for Guinevere thrilling because of the kind that it is. There is an ambiguity in Lancelot's love for Guinevere, his faithfulness being a kind of spiritual chastity, and yet for all that, a betrayal of his king and his kingdom. It is also a betrayal of himself. He will not reach Sarras, but he will become, in that mysterious chamber of the soul's dark night, the father of Galahad. 'There is no compromise with sin,' Williams writes, 'but there is every charity towards the virtues.'[4]

Finally, according to John-Manuel Andriote,

> The most clearly drawn image of Incarnation in the *Taliessin* poetry is the character of Galahad. Since Carbonek is the source of all incarnation, it is significant that Galahad is born there, for he thence issues forth as the very embodiment of

Williams' incarnationalism, and is, therefore, the amalgamation of all Williams' themes in the *Taliessin* poetry. This direct association with the place of the Hallows links Galahad to Christ and to *the* Incarnation. In light of this association, we receive Galahad as a type of the New—or renewed—Man, for Galahad is nothing less than perfect Co-inherence.[5]

As *The Son of Lancelot* opens, it is late Sunday evening in the month of February before the start of the Lenten season. It is Quinquagesima. Merlin opens mystical vision's doors with his hazel staff to reveal the first of three circles of discernment. He perceives a shrinking empire, threatened by winter wolves of two species. In the first circle are the wolves of the wild wood, howling and causing the inhabitants of Camelot to draw ever closer to the safety of their protective fires beneath multiple blankets of winter's continuously falling snows.

In the next circle, a second wolf, intruding from the east and at least as terrifying as the first, threatens the safety of the Empire with military might and denial of the Incarnation's humanity. At the circle's outer edge, Merlin sees Blanchefleur and the nuns of Almesbury. They represent earth's lambs and heaven's wolves, another example of Williams' juxtaposition of ideational division. Yet for Williams, Blanchefleur and her spiritual sisters represent the lambs' capability of accepting the influx of grace while tenacious as wolves in their determination to defend against disjunction. Blanchefleur is "the contact of exchange." Led by her, earth's lambs and heaven's wolves are the High Prince's sentinels.

Merlin sends his hearing into the vision's third sphere. Williams refers to this sphere as

> once by a northern poet [Wordsworth] beyond Snowdon [Wales/Cambria]
> seen at the rising of the moon, the *mens sensitiva*,
> the feeling intellect, the prime and vital principle,
> the pattern in heaven of Nimue,
> time's [Merlin's] mother on earth.[6]

What Merlin has entered through his auditory sense is the realm of the Third Heaven, paradise, a land of "unspeakable words."[7] It is Venus, the rising moon's first star, the sphere of divine love and the feeling intellect. Merlin hears the women's cry, the Pope's voice, and the howl of a wolf. Following the sound of the howl, Merlin enters "into sight's tritosphere" and sees the imbruted Lancelot in the form of a gaunt grey wolf, crouched upon the frozen snow and ready to pounce upon his own offspring, the newborn High Prince.

Next Williams explains the reality behind the third vision. In revealing the cause of Lancelot's imbruting, he juxtaposes time and space once again. The wounded King Pelles still suffers in Carbonek. Moreover, it is the ninth month since Lancelot, enticed to Carbonek by Nimue and drugged by Brisen, lay with the Grail princess. Upon awakening and suffering unendurable guilt for betraying Guinevere, he leaps from a window of the castle into the wintry snow and disappears into Broceliande's dark outskirts. There Lancelot's humanity dissolves into a wolverine delirium. What is left seeks to feed upon its own seed, "the seed / of love's ambiguity, love's taunt and truth."[8]

> Slavering he crouched by the dark arch of Carbonek,
> head-high howling, lusting for food, living
> for flesh, a child's flesh, his son's flesh.[9]

The Grail princess dilates and contracts, as does the Empire, while "only Lupercal and Lateran preserved Byzantium."[10] Despite the terror of the waiting wolf, the child enters the world into the waiting hands of Brisen. The High Prince, the source of humankind's second Redemption, is born.

Merlin exits the safety of Logres' gates and, to the astonished eyes of the guards, drops to all fours assuming the shape of a giant white wolf. He bounds off to Carbonek: "a white atom / spiraled wildly on the white earth, and at last / was lost."[11]

> Brisen in Helayne's chamber heard the howl
> of Lancelot, and beyond it the longer howl of the air
> that gave itself up to Merlin; she felt him come.
> She rose holding the child; the wolf and the other,
> the wind of the magical wintry beast, broke
> together on her ears; the child's mouth opened;
> his wail was a song and a sound in the third heaven.
> Down the stair of Carbonek she came to the arch
> and paused beneath; the wolf's hair rose on his hackles.
> He dragged his body nearer; he was hungry for his son.[12]

The Galahadian Ideal: Redemption Triumphant

The eighth stanza, depicting a cosmic struggle between good and evil, is pivotal in the poem's progression. On the one hand, the Emperor gathers his forces and begins to deploy them against the invading Muslims. The objective of the military campaign is to renew the allegiance of Caucasia, rescue the faith-hungry Christian refugees, meet and defeat the armies of the Prophet and destroy the Manichaean heresy. Because the campaign's ultimate goal is Incarnationalism's restoration, the Muslim and Manichaean threats to the Empire's very foundation must be destroyed; for the Empire's sake and that of western Christianity necessitates the doctrine of the Incarnation regain its place within the Divine's universal web of creation.

The second cosmic struggle, reflecting the Empire's battle on a larger stage, is the confrontation between Williams' two great lupine images. The great white wolf approaches Carbonek in his effort to gather up the infant Galahad and carry him to the safety of Blanchefleur and her sisters' arms within Almesbury's walls. The grey wolf waits in ambush, not only to destroy his lupine foe, but also to devour the fruit of his loins. Merlin's lupine image approaches Carbonek; Lancelot's image charges; the two great wolves collide in an earth-shattering joust that shakes Logres' very foundations, reverberating soundlessly beneath the winter's white dampening shroud. Good and evil collide; Lancelot is knocked unconscious; the victorious Merlin races to Brisen's waiting place beneath Carbonek's entry arch.

> [W]ith wrappings of crimson wool
> she bound the child to her crouching brother's back;
> kissed them both, and dismissed; small and asleep,
> and warm on a wolf's back, the High Prince rode into Logres.[13]

The second cosmic battle is won; the Divine's co-inherent universal web, mirrored in Logres, is on the path to redemption. Williams' pandemic imagery of Fall and Redemption, so essential to the Arthuriad's understanding, is playing out, and Redemption is within humanity's reach through Galahad's capacity for co-inherence with the One who would not save Himself.

The poem ends with Galahad's safe deliverance to Blanchefleur at Almesbury, where the child grows, cradled in the arms of the great walls. The young "Magian" is secure while his father Lancelot recovers at Carbonek. By Easter, Lancelot is healed and returns to

Logres. The poem also ends in a quatrain of unknown origin. The song glorifies Easter, the celebration of the Incarnation's triumph over death, and Galahad, humanity's reflection of its capacity for the Divine—both mirrors of deific love.

> Gaudium multum annunciamus;
> nunc in saecula servi amamus;
> civitas dulcis aedificatur;
> quia qui Amor amatur.[14]
> [We bring news of great joy;
> now in this world we servants love;
> the sweet city is being built;
> because Love who loves is being loved].[15]

The Coming of Galahad is the second turning point poem in Williams' Arthuriad dynamic. One can only speculate about Galahad's spiritual and physical upbringing within Almesbury's walls. However, when he does emerge, arriving at Camelot's court, he is recognized by all as a spiritually and physically accomplished specimen of knighthood, fixed and distinct from all the other knights.

As the poem opens, the Knights of the Round Table, including most notably Galahad, dine on the foods of their own particular choice, "an obviously psychological rather than a factual statement."[16] Thus, Williams begins the poem by suggesting a special orientation in Galahad's presence introducing "preference" as one of the poem's significant themes.

Subsequently, Galahad is led to the king's bedchamber, escorted by the king, Lancelot and the queen. The king's entire entourage follows, creating what may be interpreted as a rite of passage. When Galahad has been left to his slumber and all have retired to their rooms, the queen alone lies awake thinking only of Lancelot's son.

Once again, Taliessin, as he did in *The Crowning of Arthur,* chooses a different perspective to witness the ceremony that is unfolding before him. While Galahad is being escorted up the steep stairwell to the king's chamber, Taliessin descends to the bowels of the castle and, looking upward, follows the trail of torchlight high above. There he muses over the unfolding irony:

> He looked above; he saw
> through the unshuttered openings of stairs and rooms
> the red flares of processional torches and candles

winding to the king's bed; where instead
of Arthur Galahad that night should lie,
Helayne's son instead of the king's, Lancelot's
instead of Guinevere's, all taken at their word,
their professions, their oaths; the third heaven heard
their declarations of love, and measures them the medium of
exchange.[17]

Ridler explains: "As Galahad is set in Arthur's bed, the vows of love made by Arthur, Guinevere, and Lancelot are fulfilled by the 'third heaven,' the sphere of Venus, though not in the way they intended."[18]

Standing among the castle's jakes and latrines, Taliessin is approached by Gareth, "a prince and menial," son of Orkney's Morgause, sent to perform the castle's worst work that he might learn obedience. Gareth asks the question essential to the poem's experience, "Lord, tell me of the new knight… What man / is this for whom the Emperor lifts the Great Ban?"[19]

Among the slaves I saw from the hall's door
over the meal a mystery sitting in the air—
a cup with a covered fitting under a saffron veil,
as of the Grail itself.[20]

Consequently, Taliessin begins to answer the question posed by Gareth.

'Today the stone was fitted to the shell,' the king's poet said;
'when my lord Sir Lancelot's son sat in the perilous sell,
if he be Sir Lancelot's; in Logres the thing is done,
the thing I saw wherever I have gone—[21]

Ridler states:

C. W. explains stone and shell as the hard exploration of romantic states and the beauty of romantic states. The beauty comes before and after; which is why the shell has to be fitted to the stone to breed there, and afterwards bursts from the stone; this is the finding of identity, Galahad is the supreme of both states.[22]

Furthermore, Williams' phrase "romantic states" is pluralized, because Taliessin is about to explain Williams' geometric pattern of co-inherence's web, undimensioned and incoherent prior to Galahad's arrival, now dimensioned and co-inherent.

The romantic states consist of three concentric visions superimposed one upon the other. At the center lies the pentagram, the five-pointed mystical symbol of creation's central unity and sanctity. The inverted roofs formed by the connected vertices shelter five houses of experience. Beyond the five houses of experience lie the four zones which represent the final barrier separating the earthly Empire at the pentagram's core from the Empyrean—the Divine Mercy's and the angels' abode, Paradise.

Beginning with Williams' vision of the five houses of experience, Taliessin explores these romantic states and unveils their beauty. Each house is double in its co-inherence with the whole, having stone fitted to shell in the person of Galahad and his seating in the Siege Perilous. The first house is that of the Druid Oak, house of poetry and songs. The second house is Caucasia, the house of the flesh and roofs, representative of the exchange that lies at the source of co-inherent families. Next is the house of Gaul, seat of the intellect, proofs and theology; fourth is the altar stone of Lateran or Canterbury symbolizing the church, creeds and religion. Finally, there is Byzantium. This is the house of the porphyry stair, the kingdom and "the Acts of Identity uttered out of the Throne."[23] It is also the house of Taliessin's vision of the Empire.

Gareth responds: "And I among dung and urine—am I one / with shell or stone… in the jakes?"[24]

Taliessin responds:

> consent to be nothing but the shape in the gate of excrement,
> while Galahad in peace and the king's protection sleeps:
> question and digestion, rejection and election,
> winged shapes of the Grail's officers, double
> grand equality of the State, common of all lives,
> common of all experience, sense and more;
> adore and repent, reject and elect. Sir,
> without this alley-way how can man prefer?[25]

Taliessin's response to Gareth is clothed in the tensions of the moments that make up each day's life. He leads Gareth down the alley of synthesis, using the dialectical process, challenging him with the apparently contradictory concepts "question and digestion, rejection and election, adore and repent and reject and elect." Therefore, life consists of choices to be made. All is free will. Taliessin concludes: "and without preference can the Grail's grace be stored?"[26]

The poem's next several stanzas, lines eighty-seven through one hundred forty-five, examine preference's significance in organizing lives to serve God. The conversation is conducted among Taliessin, a slave girl and Gareth. The slave girl begins by asking the question: "Lord, / tell me the food you preferred."[27]

Answering the question, Taliessin explains that when all foods were before him, he preferred "what was there," the first thing that came to hand. Taliessin is suggesting that with free will, we enter the house of experience that lies before us. However, once the choice is made, whatever lies before us in that house's experience, "if the heart fare / stored / meats of love, laughter, intelligence, and prayer," then, it is our responsibility to accept the entered house as "best."[28] Humanity must embrace the love, laughter, intelligence and prayer offered within that house by the Divine Mercy on a moment by moment basis, grasping and embracing the moment as a gift of felicity. "It is essential throughout this discussion to remember that no one knew better than Williams the orthodox answer, that God and His service must fill the whole life."[29] Lewis states: "No doubt the general meaning is that the five houses, in each of which the shell had to be fitted to the stone, are in concrete and glorified Man brought back to unity,"[30] and Galahad is that glorified Man.

In the final stanza of the poem, Taliessin "sees the process and triumph of the soul's fruition,"[31] achievable through the fitting of the stone to the shell; Galahad taking his place upon the Siege Perilous. "This is presented in the form of an ascent to the Heaven of Heavens [Paradise, the abode of the angels and the Divine], 'the Throne's firmament,' through four planetary zones."[32] Thus, Taliessin begins his exploration and expresses appreciation for the magnitude of the four zones' beauty. The zones are the third and final circle, which encompass the central pentagram whose vertices shape the five houses' roofs and which are, in turn, ringed by the four zones, the Empyrean's frontiers. King states:

> The five zodiacal houses are Mercury, Venus, Earth [which lies within the center of the pentagram], Jupiter and Saturn. The Throne's firmament is the Earth [originally intended before

the Fall as Paradise's reflection and image] surrounded by the other zones. The first of the Sephiroth, Earth (Malkuth) is known as the kingdom: Mercury and Venus lie within the Earth's shadow in this semi-Ptolemaic scheme.[33]

Furthermore, Mercury symbolizes competition; its purpose, incoherence. In contrast, Venus, the Third Heaven, is preference's planet. Through Venus the greatest preferences offered to humankind, love and co-inherence, are attainable. With reference to Jupiter and Saturn, King further articulates:

> The astrological assumption that the planets exert influence over man is taken as an image of cosmic meaningfulness and divine providence. There is, Taliessin says, a pattern of relations among the houses, a sense of unity that may be described as "an authentic poetic vision." With these two planets, which lie beyond earth's shadow, we enter a realm beyond man's normal apprehension.[34]

Taliessin claims that Jupiter is encircled by two moons, irony and defeated irony. Irony's moon represents Lancelot's vanquishment at Carbonek, a form of human justice, while Jupiter's other moon, defeated irony, represents the victory of Blanchefleur at Almesbury where "well she nurtured Galahad," resulting in the achievement of heavenly justice. Thus Jupiter images the Divine balancing the cosmic scales of the universe. "Logres is come into Jupiter."[35] Galahad sits in the Siege Perilous and sleeps in the king's bed.

Finally, Saturn, cinctured by turned space and time—Brisen's and Merlin's plan for Logres' triumph in Galahad—is circled by Jupiter and the other planets. King states:

> The horizons come together to form a circle. Saturn was associated with contemplation and the mystic vision. In *The Divine Comedy* a golden ladder ascends from Saturn into the heavens beyond where it is lost in the mystery. Galahad represents man's capacity for wholeness. Jupiter, the present state of Logres, is the stone awaiting union with the shell, Saturn. In a moment of mystic vision, it all becomes clear to Taliessin... . That vision, however, is the poet's alone.[36]

The poem ends with Taliessin's eyes, two piercing emerald gems, reflecting hope's fulfillment and casting a "cone of energy," two "points of the Throne's foot that sank through Logres."[37] The process is complete.

The next poem in the current sequence is *Percivale at Carbonek*. The poem's twelve stanzas manifest Percivale's perspective, the third Magian in the company about to enter Carbonek. The other two Magians, Galahad and Bors, complete the main players in the poem's action. What occurs precedes the passage of the three into Carbonek's supernatural world and focuses on Galahad's last deed performed in the natural world. As such, the poem's purpose is transitional, a bridge for Galahad's crossing over to the Grail's consecrated world, symbolized by Carbonek's archway.

It is also a poem of reconciliation, a major theme of the remaining poems in this chapter. There is a certain tension in the poem as the humanity of Galahad temporarily exerts influence over his inherent perfection and grace-filled wholeness. This poignant poem, while eliciting tender and sorrowful feelings for Galahad, maintains a realistic and intellectual equilibrium.

In addition, Lewis states: "I do not know any other poet who could have conceived this scene. There are certain depths of pathos which only come to those who abstain from the more obvious and, as we say, the 'more human' forms."[38] This statement is true of much of Williams' writing and is generally accepted as a mark of his uniqueness if not his greatness. His vision perceives what many others cannot even imagine, much less articulate in words, an important characteristic of his particular creativity and capacity for developing works containing a singular literary alchemy.

As the poem opens, the Grail hovers above "in the rent saffron sun." With a saddened countenance, Galahad stands just outside Carbonek's archway and sighs for Lancelot's pardon. In Hefling's text, he recalls Williams' words, "Pardon, as between any two beings, is a re-identification of love, and it is known so in the most tender and the most happy human relationships."[39]

> Joy remembered joylessness; joy kneeled
> under the arch where Lancelot ran in frenzy [in his lupine delirium].
> The astonished angels of the spirit heard him [Galahad] moan:
> *Pardon, lord; pardon and bless me, father.*[40]

Thus, the poem commences with Galahad's plea for pardon and blessing from his father, a request for the re-identification of love between father and son.

As a last act in the natural world, Galahad, the image of "joy" and divinity, assumes a very human mien and reaches out, in humility, for his father's love. His quest for the Grail is placed on hold, as is the healing of the wounded King Pelles, until the image of joylessness and humanity, Lancelot, grants his son's unconditional pardon. Reconciliation is necessary, a very personal human need for Galahad, before he can continue his journey into the Grail's sanctified supernatural world.

Galahad kneels and weeps before Carbonek's archway as the angels, commissioned to herald his coming, watch in consternation. They are prepared to celebrate his entrance into their world, but all must await the resolution of Galahad's last human act. To paraphrase King, he, the divine, asks pardon of the human, as the human frequently entreats pardon from the Divine.[41] The Grail and the wounded king must wait while "the subdued glory [Galahad] implored the kingdom [Lancelot] / to pardon its power and the double misery of Logres [the Dolorous Blow and the destruction of the table]."[42] In this moment of tension, salvation itself hangs in the balance.

Percivale hears the padding of paws among Galahad, Bors and himself, and the "faint howl of the wolf" as "the High Prince shivered in the cold of bleak conjunction."[43] Galahad shivers because all the dichotomies to this point in the Arthuriad are upon his shoulders: Lancelot and Brisen, Arthur and Pelles, Logres and Carbonek, even humanity fallen and humanity in a state of grace. He shares in the Incarnational burden. It is a strained image since creation's salvation is at stake.

The burden is almost too great for Galahad to bear. His hands shake; his cheeks are pale; his head is a skull of sagging flesh; his dry voice rattles; he pleads, "Pardon, Lord Lancelot; pardon and blessing, father."[44] Galahad's head turns to see his father.

> the drawn engine [Lancelot]
> slewed to his left, to Bors the kin of Lancelot.
> He [Lancelot] said 'Cousin, can you bear pardon
> to the house of Carbonek from the fallen house of Camelot?'[45]

Lancelot is offering pardon and blessing to his son. Moreover, since he cannot enter Carbonek, he asks Bors to be his substitute in accepting the burden of this task.

Bors responds: "What should we forgive?" Galahad answers:
'Forgive Us,' the High Prince said, 'for Our existence;
Forgive the means of grace [Helayne] and the hope of glory [Lancelot].
In the name of Our father [Lancelot] forgive Our mother [Helayne] for Our Birth.'[46]

Bors states, "only God forgives." In doing so, he accepts the burden as an act of substitution, thus co-inhering with Lancelot, because Lancelot is "a lover and kind." Furthermore, Bors prays that his children are as accepting as he and, through God's intervention, as joyous at their birth as he was. Finally, Galahad instructs Bors to proceed through Carbonek's archway where the waiting angels embrace him. Galahad, the High Prince, follows in Bors' footprints into the warmth of the Divine Mercy's sunlight proceeding from the Grail and its overwhelming grace. Galahad's Gethsemane is ended; his perfection and wholeness are restored; the Grail's achievement and humanity's salvation are imminent.

The penultimate poem in the cosmic journey described thus far is *The Last Voyage*. The poem depicts humankind's ultimate reconciliation, embodied in Galahad, with the Divine Mercy's universal grace, suspended at the Fall. Moreover, the entire poem, especially the image of Solomon's great ship, is based largely upon portions of A. E. Waite's book, *The Hidden Church of the Holy Grail*. Mihal states:

> Williams also became involved with A. E. Waite's Order of the Golden Dawn—a semi-magical branch of Christianity known as Rosicrucianism. Rosicrucianism is a system of occult beliefs which combines the symbolism of Christianity with the terminology of Alchemy, and has the Rosy Cross as its central image. Waite had a remarkable influence on Williams. R. A. Gilbert describes the attraction of the order for Williams when he writes, 'Although he had been brought to Waite by way of the Holy Grail, Williams was most interested in Waite's kabbalistic doctrines.' Waite called Williams to his first significant contemplation of the Holy Grail as well as kabbalistic doctrines, both themes which run throughout Williams' later Arthurian poetry. The significance of Waite's influence even left one critic wondering, 'If Charles Williams had never encountered A. E. Waite and his work, would he ever have written *Taliessin through Logres* and *The Region of the Summer Stars*?'[47]

Furthermore, as to the great ship of King Solomon, Waite writes the following:

> The story of the Ship is recounted at great length, and to express it as shortly as possible, the royal prophet of Israel had learned by a message from heaven that the last knight of his lineage would exceed all other chivalry as the sun outshines the moon. By the sage counsel of his wife, he built this ship to last for 4000 years, with the double object of making known to Galahad not only the royalty of his descent, but the fact that the wise king was aware of his birth in due time... The ship was launched; the king saw in a vision how a great company of angels descended and entered therein, as it sailed far out of sight.[48]

The Last Voyage is divided into seven stanzas. The first begins with a line seemingly apart from the poem itself, "The Hollow of Jerusalem was a ship."[49] The reference is to Solomon's great mystical ship in which were placed: "King David's sword; a great bed covered with silk; a girdle made of hemp; and red, green and white spindles made from the tree Eve first planted."[50] In the poem, Solomon's vessel carries humanity's triumvirate, Galahad, Percivale and Bors, to the land of the Holy Trinity, Sarras, where, according to legend, the first among these three, Galahad, the last of David's line, achieves the Holy Grail.

Alice Mary Hadfield states, "The poem is on three levels: of poetry; of exchange, substitution, and co-inherence discovered between man and God; of the Grail and King Arthur."[51] While the poem may be evaluated in its pure poetic form and in the matter of Arthur's interaction with the Grail, its level of the co-inherence discovered between man and God confirms its true relevance to Williams' vision of humankind's cosmic journey.

The poem's first stanza sets the mood for what is to follow. There is an apparent strained, stressed and tense atmosphere. Williams uses the following expression to establish that mood:

> But the actual ship, the hollow of Jerusalem,
> beyond the shapes of empire, the capes of Carbonek,
> over the topless waves of trenched Broceliande,
> drenched by the everlasting spray of existence,
> with no mind's sail reefed or set, no slaves at the motivated oars,
> drove into and clove the wind from unseen shores.[52]

The ship seems rudderless, driven by the forces of nature to a distant, unknown destination. However, King suggests that "a sense of destination is conveyed through the image of a 'knotted web of empire' and through the paradoxical description of the web being 'multiple without dimension, indivisible without uniformity.'"[53]

The third stanza's main theme centers round the use of the word "alchemical" to describe Galahad. Traditionally, the word conveys the belief that a base metal, for example lead, can be transformed into a precious metal, gold, through alchemical processes. However, the word as used by Williams represents not merely a physical transmutation, but a spiritual one as well. The transmutation he suggests is one of humanity's finite physical mortality metamorphosing into infinite spiritual immortality. This is Galahad's special gift as humankind's surrogate before the Divine Mercy. Through the alchemical process' spiritual dimension, he is capable of co-inhering with the Divine, imaging humankind's potential to do the same.

> The fourth stanza opens with the phenomenon of
> [a]n infinite flight of doves from the storming sky
> of Logres—strangely sea-travelers when the land melts—
> forming to overfeather and overwhelm the helm,
> numerous as men in the empire, the empire riding
> the skies of the ocean, guiding by modulated stresses
> on each spoke of the helm the vessel from the realm of Arthur,
> lifted oak and elm to a new-ghosted power.[54]

The anomaly of doves replacing gulls in the skies over the sea is too apparent to be casually dismissed. Williams is injecting a special insight into the scene; the doves are the Holy Spirit's presence guiding the travelers upon their leagueless voyage and the City unraveling the "knotted web of empire" on this passage of discovery.

Further, the essence formed by the doves guides the hands of Galahad that are reeved on the prow while "the ban and blessing of the empire ran in his arms."[55] Under Galahad's stewardship and in co-inherence with the Divine Mercy, humanity's fall is overcome and redemption achieved. Hadfield states: "Galahad, doing the work of steering the ship, was fulfilling a potentiality in man to reach perfection."[56]

Stanzas five and six deal with Blanchefleur and Dinidan respectively. Blanchefleur is borne upon Solomon's ship to her final resting place at Sarras. The triumvirate recognizes Blanchefleur as exchange's perfection. Her honor is to lie in the sacred ground of the Holy Trinity. In contrast, Dinidan, "the king's dolphin," suffers death's infamy, burned at the stake at Morgause's sons' hands. Gawaine and Agravaine also kill their mother, Morgause, and their mother's lover, Lamorack. But only Dinadan's death elicits the following response from Galahad:

> But the Infant's [Galahad's] song was thick with a litany of names from the king and the king's friend to the least of the slaves. He [Dinidan] was borne through the waves to his end on a cry of substitution.[57]

Thus, exchange is honored and substitution is implemented, as the pattern of co-inherence is further enhanced between humanity and the Divine through the persons of Galahad and his small company of fellow travelers on this limitless odyssey of reconciliation.

The penultimate poem's next to last stanza captures reconciliation's crucial concept, synergy with the Divine throughout eternity. The "omnipotent fact rushed the act of Galahad,"[58] for God energizes Galahad's mission to heal King Pelles. With the energy absorbed by Galahad, he sings into the wind as his ancestor, David, had done on numerous occasions millennia before. However, this time David's descendent, in a synergetic state of ecstasy with the Divine, sings not the words "*Judica me, Deus,*"[59] but rather "*Judica te, Deus.*"[60] "In the monstrum [suggestive of the monstrance used to display the Host/Eucharist during the Benediction in the Catholic tradition] of triangular speed,"[61] the Fact, the Father, the Flesh, the Incarnate Son and Intelligence, the Holy Spirit, and the co-inherent Holy Trinity receive Galahad into David's co-inherent royal lineage. Therefore, from God to David, David to Solomon, Solomon to Christ, through the Father's special indulgence, and from Christ to Galahad, "the necessity of being was communicated to the son of Lancelot."[62] The derived being, Galahad, is brought into full understanding of the Necessary Being through the Divine Mercy's extraordinary grace.

Thus, when Galahad challenges God to judge Himself, essentially, he is challenging himself to be judged by God, because he is in unity with the Holy Trinity. In his essay "The Cross," Williams argues:

This then is the creation that 'needs' (let the word be permitted) justifying. The Cross justifies it to this extent at least—that just as He submitted us to His inexorable will, so He submitted Himself to our wills (and therefore to His). He made us; He maintained us in our pain. At least, however, on the Christian showing, He consented to be Himself subject to it. If, obscurely, He would not cease to preserve us in the full horror of existence, at least He shared it. He became as helpless as we under the will which is He. This is the first approach to a sense of justice in the whole situation. Whatever He chose, He chose fully, for Himself as for us. This is, I think, unique in the theistic religions of the world. I do not remember any other in which the Creator so accepted His own terms—at least in the limited sense of existence upon this earth. It is true that His life was short. His pains (humanly speaking) comparatively brief. But at least, alone among the gods, He deigned to endure the justice He decreed.[63]

In the final stanza, the legend's last exchange is completed. Arthur is dead, the regicide committed by his son, Modred. King Pelles is healed, the healing realized with Galahad's achievement of the Holy Grail. The death and healing occur simultaneously. Williams proclaims: "[T]he two kings were one, by exchange and healing. / Logres was withdrawn to Carbonek; it became Britain."[64]

Just as the body and blood of Christ are inexorably integrated into the chalice's molecular structure, to exist for all eternity since nothing can end that is created by God; so, too, Galahad is assimilated into the Grail's crucial principles, attaining perfection's image for humanity to emulate. The cosmic journey of mankind is ended; the allegorical concordance of Galahad and the Grail with the Holy Trinity at Sarras is consummated; the Second Redemption is realized.

Taliessin at Lancelot's Mass is the last poem in the Galahadian ideal's final triumph and the last of Williams' Arthurian cycle. It is interesting to note that he began the Grail journey with his novel, *War in Heaven*, which reaches its climax in a mass celebrated by Prester John, and he concludes the journey with a poem whose themes center around a mass celebrated by Lancelot.

The two masses are very similar in character, celebrating the Divine Mercy's communal unity. In each, the central character is appropriated into the Divine Mercy's elegant grace, Galahad in the former work and the Archdeacon in the latter. Finally, the souls of the departed in Christ are summoned to attendance and participate equally in the commemoration.

Taliessin is once again the observer and reporter of events. However, in this instance, and in contrast to previous poems in which he fulfilled these roles, he also is an active participant. He is second only to Galahad in intuiting the conceptual thread conjoining all the poem's elements; humanity's co-inherence with the Incarnation's birth, death and Resurrection through the achievement of the Holy Grail.

Time is irrelevant to the poem's structural theme. Once again, Williams suspends time, for what is pertinent to the poem has no beginning and no end; it is eternal. The Mass is the focus of that eternity stretching backward and forward simultaneously, just as there is no beginning and no end to the Creation, which exists in the mind of the Father and thus, is eternal by its very existence in the Godhead.

Clearly what Williams is really proposing in this poem is the church's realization of time's irrelevance with reference to the Parousia. It is evident that the Second Coming is not occurring momentarily. Therefore, the church's response is the Second Coming's celebration through the Sacramental Eucharist within the paradigmatic ceremony of the Mass' liturgy. King states:

> When it became clear that the Second coming would be indefinitely delayed, the church accepted the conditions imposed by time and continued to celebrate the Presence under the form of Bread and Wine, types of the Body and Blood, and to pursue in the everyday world the way of substitution and exchange that the Sacrament affirmed and empowered. "Taliessin at Lancelot's Mass" is an explication of that change of method.[65]

King further suggests:

> God, whose power is not limited by human categories, gathers all time around the one Center, the resurrection of the Incarnate Word. God's grace, not limited by the accident of time, reaches both backward and forward, stretching from eternity to eternity.[66]

This interpretation is not new to King, and he does not claim it to be, for it is expounded at great length and specific detail in

Williams' masterful theological work, *The Descent of the Dove*, Chapter Two, "The Reconciliation with Time."

As the poem opens, the Mass occurs within the context of several events. First, there is a description of the altar upon which the celebration takes place. Also, the celebrant, Lancelot, one "not sworn of the priesthood," appears in knight's armor but without helmet, sword or mailed gloves. Second, the deceased knights of the Round Table are in attendance, standing between "Nimue of Broceliande and Helayne of Carbonek." At the same time, Guinevere is in Blanchefleur's cell at Almesbury and suffers from the pangs of lost motherhood. The queen's substitution through her suffering allows the wounded and dead king to enter "into salvation to serve the Grail." Pelles moves to the altar and Arthur steps down, once again recreating a scene from Prester John's Mass, as Adrian and the Archdeacon exchange places, the former descending from the altar while the latter ascends in substitution's act to die in exchange for the life of the child and in unity with the unfolding transcendent experience.

Finally, Williams states, "the unseen knight of terror stood as a friend."[67] For him, the unseen knight is the presence of the Holy Spirit "as It exercises Its operations in the world."[68] Contrary to earlier interpretations of the unseen or Invisible Knight,[69] King suggests:

> "The Invisible Knight, then, is that good that man by nature seeks, but which after the Dolorous Blow he sees not at all or partially distorted... To man's eyes, distorted by the Fall, the knight seems the opposite of what he actually is, and also the opposite of what unregenerate man thinks he wants. Only when the sky turns around and new light breaks does he appear in his normal guise.... With the recognition of the Invisible Knight, events move toward consummation.[70]

At this point the mass continues with the Byzantine Rite's Epiclesis, the invocation of the Holy Spirit in consecrating the Eucharist's Bread and Wine. As the Host is raised, the image's singular Unity is exalted; the Unity's prism reflects the web of co-inherence, its paths and points consolidating the core substance within the Unity, much as, in *The Coming of Galahad*, the pentagram's points are connected by paths creating a web of interrelationships and interdependence. The Holy Spirit's flame appears over the altar, and Galahad and the Table are assumed into Its living essence, the two glories intertwined. In a parallel perspective of the mass celebrated in *War in Heaven*, Prester John and the Grail are assumed into the living universe's infinite expansion of stars and heavenly bodies.

The poem's focal point follows: "interchanged adoration, interdispersed prayer, / the ruddy pillar of the Infant was the passage of the porphyry / stair."[71] With these lines, Williams implies the following question: What then is the achievement of the Grail? In *The Figure of Arthur,* he answers:

> Dante, in a later century, was to put the height of human beatitude in the understanding of the Incarnation; in a lesser, but related method, Angela of Foligno was to speak of knowing 'how God comes into the Sacrament.' To know these things is to be native to them; to live in the world where the Incarnation and the Sacrament (single or multiple) happen. It is more: it is, in some sense, to live beyond them, or rather (since that might sound profane) to be conscious of them as one is conscious of oneself, Christ-conscious instead of self-conscious. The achievement of the Grail is the perfect fulfillment of this, the thing happening.[72]

The final three stanzas center upon Taliessin. His mission ended, manacled by the web, he is, at the same time, paradoxically free. His poetry is no longer capable of expressing his joy, for any joy his poetry heretofore expressed was in search of the unknown Joy. However, the Joy manifested makes his songs superfluous. Taliessin returns to his origins and leaves the rest to the Company he leaves behind.

In his article, "Charles Williams and the Arthurian Tradition," McClatchey states:

> In what is artistically Williams's final Arthurian poem… Taliessin experiences in the Holy Eucharist a consciousness of the Incarnation and the Sacrament so acute that he feels himself to be completely at one with the Mysteries. It is the supreme moment of his life and doubtless… the summit of Williams's lifelong calling, as it combines the Arthurian, Taliessinic, and Eucharistic traditions… .
>
> Suddenly we realize that Charles Williams has given us a new Grail hero, for Taliessin has indeed Achieved the Grail. This is the secret hidden in the very operation of Williams's handling of the Arthurian materials, because he faithfully

sought always whatever was central, and finding thereby a new definition of the Achievement of the Grail, found also thereby a new Grail achiever, Taliessin.

Finally, Williams speaks of Galahad being assumed into the Grail. May we not now fairly tell of Taliessin being assumed into the Myth, the Grail into the Holy Eucharist, and the Eucharist into Christ? For all of these have been artistically assumed into the poetry that Williams left us, thereby raising each one of us through his poetic vision to a new understanding of true grace and beauty.[73]

Let true grace and beauty be also known as God and His Creation.

---

[1] Ridler 58.
[2] Williams, "Notes" 176.
[3] Williams, "Malory" 189.
[4] King 88.
[5] Andriote 77.
[6] Williams and Lewis, *Taliessin*, "The Son of Lancelot" L53-56.
[7] *Holy Bible*, 2 Cor. 12:2-4.
[8] Williams and Lewis, *Taliessin*, "Son of Lancelot" L94-95.
[9] Ibid. L99-101.
[10] Ibid. L110.
[11] Ibid. L165-168.
[12] Ibid. L178-187.
[13] Ibid. L212-215.
[14] Ibid. L254-257.
[15] Ridler 60.
[16] King 95.
[17] Williams and Lewis, *Taliessin*, "The Coming of Galahad" L14-23.
[18] Ridler 64.
[19] Williams and Lewis, *Taliessin*, "Galahad" L37, 46-47.
[20] Ibid. L43-46.
[21] Ibid. L62-66.
[22] Ridler 65.
[23] Williams and Lewis, *Taliessin*, "Galahad" L72.
[24] Ibid. L74-75.
[25] Ibid. L77-86.
[26] Ibid. L86.
[27] Ibid. L87-88.
[28] Ibid. L115-16.

29 Williams and Lewis 354.
30 Ibid. 354.
31 Ibid. 355.
32 Ibid. 355.
33 King 101.
34 Ibid. 102.
35 Williams and Lewis, *Taliessin*, "Galahad" L160.
36 King 102.
37 Williams and Lewis, *Taliessin*, "Galahad" L164.
38 Williams and Lewis 361.
39 Hefling 58.
40 Williams and Lewis, *Taliessin*, "Percivale at Carbonek" L5-8.
41 King 112.
42 Williams and Lewis, *Taliessin*, "Percivale" L15-16.
43 Ibid. L24.
44 Ibid. L28.
45 Ibid. L33-36.
46 Ibid. L37-41.
47 Mihal xv.
48 Waite 301, 303.
49 Williams and Lewis, *Taliessin*, "The Last Voyage" L1.
50 Mihal 271.
51 Ridler 75.
52 Williams and Lewis, *Taliessin*, "Voyage" L20-25.
53 King 115.
54 Williams and Lewis, *Taliessin*, "Voyage" L46-52.
55 Ibid. L67.
56 Ridler 76.
57 Williams and Lewis, *Taliessin*, "Voyage" L96-100.
58 Ibid. L106.
59 *Holy Bible*, Psalm 43.
60 Williams and Lewis, *Taliessin*, "Voyage" L109.
61 Ibid. L116.
62 Ibid. L118.
63 Williams, "The Cross" 132.
64 Williams and Lewis, *Taliessin*, "Voyage" L124-125.
65 King 120.
66 Ibid. 121.
67 Williams and Lewis, *Taliessin*, "Taliessin at Lancelot's Mass" L23.
68 Williams and Lewis 270.
69 see Malory ii, 14, 16.
70 King 122.
71 Williams and Lewis, *Taliessin*, "Lancelot's Mass" L48.
72 Williams and Lewis 262-263.
73 McClatchey, "Charles Williams" 61.

Chapter 8

Charles Williams' Literary Achievement

Charles Williams died on Tuesday, May 15, 1945. He had entered Radcliffe Infirmary in Oxford to undergo what was considered to be minor surgery. He did not survive. C. S. Lewis states:

> We, his male friends at Oxford, had had no notion that he was even ill until we heard that he was in the Radcliffe Infirmary; nor did we then suspect that the trouble was serious. I heard of his death at the Infirmary itself, having walked up there with a book I wanted to lend him, expecting this news that day as little (almost) as I expected to die that day myself. It was a Tuesday morning, one of our times of meeting. I thought he would have given me messages to take on to the others. When I joined them with my actual message… I had some difficulty making them believe or even understand what had happened. The world seemed to us at that moment primarily a *strange* one… [Perhaps Charles Williams' death] is best understood in the light of some words that one of his friends said to me as we sat in Addison's Walk just after the funeral. 'Our Lord told the disciples it was expedient for them that He should go away for otherwise the Comforter would not come to them. I do not think it blasphemous to suppose that what was true archetypally, and in eminence, of His death may, in the appropriate degree, be true of the deaths of all His followers.'
>
> So, at any rate, many of us felt it to be. No event has so corroborated my faith in the next world as Williams did simply by

dying. When the idea of death and the idea of Williams thus met in my mind, it was the idea of death that was changed.

He was buried in St. Cross churchyard... .[1]

Essentially, Lewis is commenting on Charles Williams' steadiness of spirit and depth of heart, so widely perceived with affection and love by those with whom he shared his life.

An article by T. S. Eliot, titled "The Significance of Charles Williams," appeared in *The Listener* in December, 1946, a little over a year after Williams' death. In it, Eliot attempts to explain why Williams is unfairly underrated as a writer.

> There are two reasons why Charles Williams has not been fully appreciated. First... hardly any of his work is quite perfect as literary art. Williams was something more uncommon than a literary artist. Second, the capacity for recognizing the realities to which Williams was trying to draw our attention is numbed and almost atrophied in the world in which we live today. [As true in 2014 as it was in 1946.] If this capacity is latent in you, Williams is the writer to bring it to consciousness. I do not mean simply that Williams was a Christian writer, and that the world has ceased to be Christian. It is not so simple as that. There are many good Christians today who believe in spiritual reality but have no experience of it: their Christianity is rather an aspiration than an awareness. To be brought face to face with what Williams saw, is as much the need in our time, for those who call themselves Christians, as it is for everyone else.[2]

This quotation by Eliot emphasizes Williams' power as a writer. He is unclassifiable. He cannot be pigeonholed into a tiny compartment and left there to slide into unwarranted obscurity, even though many attempts have been made to relegate him to that state. Debates as to whether he is a major or minor writer continue to this day. However, to proceed in this direction is to do great disservice to Williams' work, for he is neither of these. Moreover, even Thomas Howard, leading authority on Williams' novels, conveys the impression that the label "major" may be too small to fit Williams.[3]

Then what is he? He is a visionary, unrestrained by literary convention and thus free to exercise a soaring imagination encompassing awareness of a reality which others can only aspire to, but never achieve; a reality far beyond the frontiers of human experience. Williams' reality, however, is consummated within his very consciousness.

War in Heaven and the *Arthuriad* are fundamentally an extended metaphor tracing humankind's fall from grace and the struggle to regain that grace. As such, the journey is a cosmic experience expressed through the Grail Quest mythology, and the Grail's Achievement is the metaphorical attainment of Paradise.

Subsequently, upon entering Paradise, humanity sees and experiences the phenomenon of God as only a co-inherent soul can. Assimilated into the Holy Trinity's nature, the souls of all the faithful are cognizant of the spiritual realities that represent the truth, beauty and wisdom that are God and His creation. This is Williams' spiritual realm and awareness.

Susan Wendling agrees with Eliot that only those who are diligently searching for spiritual veracity, free from deceit and falseness, can experience Williams' essence and be free to enjoy his reality's magnificent vistas. She states that he offers "great beauty and intellectual significance to the searching mind," and she emphasizes "how central 'the Grail Quest' was not only to Charles Williams' poetic achievement but also to his spiritual vision."[4]

Furthermore, Mary Dugan, in commenting upon his literary art, states unequivocally: "Williams was not a writer who happened to be a Christian, but a Christian who chose to express the "awakening, insight and universality which are the qualities of true art."[5] She goes on to explain:

> He recognized that the entire created order holds importance only as it relates to and expresses God, who has brought it into being. This is the source of meaning and primary relationship for all being... For Williams, the life of Jesus Christ is a 'pageant of the events of the human soul,' a pattern for our own realization of the divine life in us and of the kingdom of heaven which is our birthright... This creative fusion of Christian doctrine with poetic images frees Williams' Arthurian poetry from the humanistic limitations and emotional excesses that flaw others' treatment of the matter... He involves us in specific and exact images that shatter our mental limitations, causing us to experience God and His creation as immediate and alive... .[6]

Dugan is commenting upon one of the overlooked gems manifested in all Williams' works, namely a wisdom that is characterized by warmth, tangible charity, and love, creating in readers the possibilities for a "new Eden." A mind open to his reality experiences both the potentiality for judging rightly in matters relating to life and conduct, as well as the integrity of reasoning from premises and general principles in the choice of means and ends. His wisdom is based upon the three foundations of his spiritual vision: the Incarnation, Crucifixion and Resurrection of the Divine Mercy, Jesus Christ, the Father's Beloved Son and His Mediator with the sons and daughters of Adam. Additionally, it is the spiritual reality of all these miraculous events embraced in the Sacramental Eucharist having at its core the Grail of salvation, which "absorbed something of the high intensity of the moment when it was used."[7] Thus, for Williams, the Achievement of the Grail is also the achievement of wisdom based upon Christ-consciousness rather than any self-consciousness.

> Moreover, for Dugan:
>   It is the breadth of the poet's vision which inspires respect. We are not, in this century, accustomed to what poet Edwin Muir referred to as 'a great theme greatly treated.' Most of us... have been too absorbed in our own small worlds. Charles Williams invades this smallness and puts it to shame by holding in his consciousness, simultaneously, a network of relationships between some of the most profound truths of Christian faith and mythology as fundamental to us as the very roots of our speech. Indeed, we would best approach Williams... with one thought in mind—the gaining of wisdom. In this we will not be disappointed.[8]

In his essay, "The World of Arthur and the Grail in the Work of Charles Williams," Karl Heinz Goller presents a different approach to Williams' significance, critiquing his literary art within a modernist paradigm. For example, Goller states:

> The present day reader will find Williams 'modern' where features of his style lead to esoteric ambiguity and to indirection in respect to the poetic meaning; the manneristic interlacing of convoluted patterns, the juxtaposition of disparate metaphors. But in contrast to other modern poets [and

writers], the enigmatization of the message is oriented towards the topic and upon closer study cryptic obscurity gives way to the sharp contours of objective clarity.[9]

With Williams' use of convolution and juxtaposition as literary techniques in dealing with disconnected metaphors, Goller recognizes a thoroughly modern writer. Perhaps this observation's best example occurs in the scene at the "White Mass" in *War in Heaven*, when Lionel and Barbara, along with the Duke, see beyond Prester John, as he lifts the Grail,

> the moving universe of stars, and then one flying planet, and then fields and rooms and a thousand remembered places, and all in light and darkness and peace. He seemed to hold the Grail no more; the divine colour that moved in that vision of creation swathed Him as a close-bound robe.[10]

Goller further explains:

> For this poet, the world of the Grail is not merely part of an ancient and venerable myth; it is an intellectual challenge, and a catalyst for concentration and reflection. Thus the Grail remains a symbol of the transcendental mystery, but the message Williams imbues it with has nothing to do with the a-logical fascination of modern lyric poetry. Even those who do not respond to the message, who find it old fashioned, unrealistic and without appeal, cannot but admit that the poetic world created by Williams is coherent, comprehensible, and consistent.[11]

In the quote above, Goller points out why Williams' critics cannot deny how harmonious and fathomable he is. He does not treat the Grail myth as simply a myth. Rather, using it as a springboard to a higher understanding, he seeks to resolve the intellectual challenge he finds there, utilizing the myth as an agent for convergence and contemplation upon the transcendent mystery that is the Grail.

What is that great mystery? In the words of his most famous epigram, "This also is Thou, neither is this Thou." In its absorbed energy, the Last Supper's Holy Grail represents consciousness of Christ's Incarnation, Crucifixion and Resurrection. At the same time, it is a created vessel which, in its archetypal role, points to a metaphysical ideal existing beyond empirical knowledge, but not beyond the boundaries of our collective imaginations, and certainly not beyond Charles Williams' individual imagination.

Goller goes on:

> The anticipation of an atheistic, secular rejection of such a Christian work by skeptics sometimes leads to an apologetic, almost polemic stance on the part of sympathetic critics—one that Williams hardly requires.
>
> Indeed, the world of Williams is modern, vibrant with dynamic motion and spiritual anxiety. It is a portrait of mankind threatened by forces and powers of destruction. In spite of the poet/writer's adherence to... medieval sources, the material has become a vehicle for a message of the twentieth century. This may well be due to the fact that Charles Williams has gained a deeper understanding of Arthurian mythology than any of his predecessors, and because he has given poetic voice to truths of which they were only subconsciously aware.[12]

What is Williams' message for the twenty-first century? His vision and personal experience are conscious of an interrelationship and interdependence bestowed upon all God's creation through His special grace; and because creation reflects His image, the universe, even though infinite and immeasurable, is itself an image of that model. Moreover, what God knows cannot exist outside Him. Therefore, within the Creator's infinite knowledge, there is the same conscious pattern for His creation: a mirror reflecting Creation's potential for co-inherence through substitution and exchange. These represent God's answer to humanity's questions, "Who am I, and why am I here?" This is Williams' constancy, his literary achievement for which so many other poets/writers search and never find the answer.

Goller concludes:

> Williams, as a poet, has yet to come into his own. Some of the best minds of this century—among them fellow writers and friends, such as T. S. Eliot, Dorothy Sayers, Anne Ridler, and John Heath-Stubbs—have recognized the profundity and the enormous scope of his vision. The scholar and friend who was closest to him—C. S. Lewis—has told us how to gauge the

poetic achievement of "Taliessin through Logres" and "The Region of the Summer Stars":

'They seem to me, both for the soaring and gorgeous novelty of their technique and for their profound wisdom, to be among the two or three most valuable books of verse produced in the century.'[13]

At this juncture, it is appropriate to consider Williams' use of the medium of Grail mythology. Previously, I have argued that Williams utilized the myth as "a catalyst for concentration and reflection" upon the transcendent mystery that is the Grail. Why does he believe that mythology can perform this function?

In a letter to Liza Marian Butler, dated September 25, 1940, C. S. Lewis, Williams' closest friend, colleague and intellectual collaborator, makes the following observation about mythology:

Mythologies and religions are products of imagination in the sense that their content is *imaginative*. The more *imaginative* ones are 'nearer the mark' in the sense that they communicate more Reality to us. Poetry 'creates life' in the sense that its products are something more than fictions occurring in human minds, mere psychological phenomena, and can therefore be described as inhabiting a 'spiritual world.' Poets 'proclaim the mystery' in the sense that they somehow convey to us an inkling of supersensual and super-intellectual Reality: which is a mystery in the sense of *mysterium tremendum*, something not merely which we happen not to know but which transcends our common modes of perception. They produce the illusion of penetrating it in the sense that they make us feel we have *understood* when we have really been refreshed by contact of quite a different kind with Reality. [Mythological] poetry is a great power in the sense of actually enriching our deepest life by such contacts.[14]

Thus, Lewis identifies several possibilities for Williams' use of mythology as a prism for meditation upon the Grail's transcendent mystery. First, it is an extraordinarily imaginative approach to dealing with an epic mystery. Second, mythology's use enables the poet/writer to expose the reader to a spiritual world of "super-sensual and super-intellectual Reality." Third, the mythological approach also enables the reader to transcend "common modes of perception" which encourage the illusion of understanding. However, what is authentic is an inspiriting contact with Reality that only enriches "our deepest life" and the very breath for our immortal souls.

In Charles Moorman's *Arthurian Triptych: Mythic Materials in Charles Williams, C. S. Lewis, and T. S. Eliot*, the author states:

> Myth itself represents an ultimate and absolute reality; myth in literature represents a reflection of that reality, a shadowy and sometimes distorted reflection of that reality to be sure, but nearly always capable of conveying the meaning and, to some extent, the power implicit in the myth itself. Lewis implies both in his statements on myth, and in his own allusions to myth, that myth functions in literature as a suggestive archetype to which ordinary fictional situations may be referred by allusion. In this way, myth lends its own total meaning and inherent power to the fictional situation.[15]

In the end, mythical structure's use in fiction gives verisimilitude and integrity to the actions portrayed in the closely examined work.

King explains the importance of Williams' use of mythology for the contemporary reader when he states:

> I have permitted it [Williams' poetry] to speak for itself... as part of a larger, coherent, skillfully executed vision of Williams's sense of what is real in human experience. The vision itself is intelligently conceived and, although expressed largely in terms of Christian theology, its scope, depth, and inclusiveness transcends sectarianism to become universal myth. It makes a statement beyond parochial limits.
>
> It is more than just a statement, however. Expressed in a form that is emotional and sensuous as well as intellectual, it becomes poetry—the most comprehensive kind of poetry, mythical. Grounded on insights and values that are universal and timeless, it represents one effort in the twentieth century to perpetuate a continuing poetic tradition in a structure that speaks meaningfully to the contemporary reader.[16]

Systematically analyzing Williams' poetry, King concludes that the structure of Williams' works emphasizes poignancy, promotes aesthetic pleasure and, at the same time, challenges the intellect. For him, this is the most sweeping literary achievement that a poet/writer can attain—mythical poetry. As such, it represents one effort to present to the twenty-first-century reader a perpetually "continuing poetic tradition."

Thus far, this examination of Williams' *War in Heaven* and *Arthuriad* has scrutinized the distinctive and unique elements they contain. None are more important than the elements of wisdom, modernity and mythology investigated in this chapter. However, in Williams' world, a fourth element, perhaps the most significant one, spirituality, merits specific attention.

This element requires a working definition, for spirituality can mean many things to many people. James Mackey provides a thoughtful and precise definition in the preface to *Celtic Spirituality*, edited and translated by Oliver Davies. Mackey states:

> *Spirituality* is a word that is not always to everyone's liking. This is partly because, in the Age of Heroic Materialism, still hugely influential all about us, the word *spirit* and its derivatives seem to be reminiscent of a dualistic and obsolescent Christian Platonism and the negative aura set over this word by some of its determined practitioners... [Also] spirituality seems to require and to invite us to seek out and cultivate very esoteric kinds of inner experience that have little or nothing to do with marrying, begetting and rearing children, harvesting land and sea, and the myriad other activities that crowd together under these comprehensive references to making a living, or getting a life here and now in the only world we know for sure to exist...
>
> The most effective way of rescuing spirituality from such unwelcome misapprehensions, then, is to present to the public a world in which... spirit never leaves and never will leave the body. This is a world of eternally immanent, incarnate spirit—spirit that transcends the whole universe of being toward the ultimate and eternal perfection of the universe, precisely because it is immanent in the whole of it.[17]

This is exactly Williams' point in all he wrote. Spirituality cannot be separated from everyday life; it is Creation's nucleus. Since marriage, begetting and rearing children and a legion of additional human activities are a fundamental irreducible constituent of Creation's perfection, spirituality is the thread binding all humanity into the woven fabric of everyday life's activities.

Can we deny the Holy Family's spirituality as it went about its business living everyday life? Can we deny the spirituality of Bors' Elayne, when he states in *Bors to Elayne; on the King's Coins*:

> Now when the thumbs are muscled with the power of good will
> corn comes to the mill and the flour to the house,
> bread of love for your women and my men;
> at the turn of the day, and none only to earn;
> in the day of the turn, and none only to pay;
> for the hall is raised to the power of exchange for all,
> by the small spread of organisms of your hands; O Fair,
> there are the altars of Christ the City extended?[18]

Is this not spirituality expressed in everyday living?

Then there is the plight of Lester and Richard in Williams' novel, *All Hallows' Eve*. Lester, after dying in a plane crash, realizes she never truly appreciated her husband, Richard, while alive. Now, however, in the realm of the spirits, which Williams believes exists just beyond humanity's ken, like the Celtic "thin places," Lester sees Richard in the pure light of their shared spirituality. Williams portrays spirituality's poignancy and the affect it has in the following scene when, for a moment, the two worlds intersect as Williams believes happens more frequently than realized through the grace of the Divine Mercy:

> He added, across the room to Lester, without surprise, but with a rush of apology, and only he knew to whom he spoke, "Darling, have I kept you waiting? I'm so sorry."
>
> Lester saw him. She felt, as he came, all her old self lifting in her; bodiless, she seemed to recall her body in the joy they exchanged. He saw her smile, and in the smile heaven was frank and she was shy. She said—and he only heard, and he rather knew than heard, but some sound of speech rang in the room... she said, 'I'll wait for you a million years.' She felt a stir within her, as if life quickened; and she remembered with new joy that the deathly tide had never reached, even in appearance, to the physical house of life. If Richard or she went now, it would not much matter; their fulfillment was irrevocably promised them, in what manner so-ever they knew or were to know it.[19]

Here is complementary spirituality experienced across the frontier of two matrices of reality within Creation's macrocosm. It is spirituality within sacramental marriage's pattern, which death itself cannot dissolve, demonstrating the bond that that act of sacred union has within the spiritual entity of two very ordinary people's lives in the here and the hereafter.

In conclusion, one may justifiably ask, "What does this study contribute to understanding Charles Williams' place within recent literary history?" The primary goal of this work is to determine whether Charles Williams deserves more than a cursory acknowledgment for his literary efforts. In the process of examining the proposition, a vast panorama of new and exciting discoveries arose. His poetry, represented by *Taliessin through Logres* and *The Region of the Summer Stars*, and his fiction, represented by the novel, *War in Heaven*, emphasize the numinous meaning of the Holy Grail. However, close investigation of Williams' Holy Grail concept clearly exposes his entire theological paradigm. For him, the Grail legend becomes the means for envisaging a greater theological pattern.

Moreover, Williams does not browbeat with his beliefs. Rather, he gradually leads the reader to develop conclusions about their validity by sharing his vision of what he perceives as three distinct realities: Divine Truth, Divine Beauty and Divine Wisdom. It is for the reader to try to understand the vision and to delimitate the import of the three realities.

What then is Charles Williams' vision, authenticating his literary achievement and validating his unrestrained imagination in presenting his spiritual paradigm? First, he introduces a nonpareil conception of the infinite universe's co-inherent configuration. Second, he proposes that universe's truth, which is God the Father and His gift of grace conferred upon Adam and his children through the Creation. Next, he presents the beauty of the Incarnated Son, begotten through the Blessed Virgin's imbuing by the Holy Spirit. The Son is the Father's second offering to humanity: a sacrificial lamb, a gift from the Father to his fallen children and an avenue for their redemption. He is the Divine Mercy, the most beautiful countenance in all Creation, laid at Adam's children's feet.

In Williams' vision, the co-inherent configuration's final reality is wisdom. It is wisdom centered upon understanding the integrity of Creation's complex pattern, an integrity founded upon substitution and exchange and witnessed throughout Creation. It binds the whole, where there is no beginning and no end, with sublime interrelatedness and interdependence.

Thus, Charles Williams, through his literary technique's modernity, with mythology's catalytic capability for concentration and reflection, and spirituality's boundless grace, brings the reader to the porphyry stair. Ascending the stair, the reader confronts the door opening upon Williams' vision of Creation's form supported by its tri-Realities: Truth, Beauty and Wisdom. Passing through the door, the reader encounters eternity's reflection, Charles Williams' vision of the Holy Trinity's Transcendent Reality. His illimitable imagination reveals a measureless insight into the co-inherent unity of Creation's Father, Christianity's Incarnate Son and Civilization's Holy Spirit of Wisdom.

---

[1] Lewis xiii-xiv
[2] Eliot 895.
[3] Howard 289-290.
[4] Wendling 2, 7.
[5] Dugan 86.
[6] Ibid. 87, 91-93.
[7] Williams, *War* 37.
[8] Dugan 94.
[9] Goller 171.
[10] Williams, *War* 254.
[11] Goller. 171-172.
[12] Ibid. 172-173.
[13] Ibid. 173.
[14] Hooper 445.
[15] Moorman 125.
[16] King 166.
[17] Davies xv.
[18] Williams and Lewis, *Taliessin*, "King's Coins" L21-28.
[19] Williams. *All Hallows Eve* 169.

Acknowledgements

I would like to acknowledge the following people who have played an important role in the completion of this book. I owe more than I can ever repay to Dr. James Pain for introducing me to Charles Williams, for his hours of listening to and hearing what I was trying to say about C. W., for his insightful commentary and gentle nudging and, finally, for the pleasant lunches we shared at Charlie Brown's. I am blessed with a truly remarkable and inspiring mentor and friend.

If the writing in this work is clear and articulate, it is due to Dr. Virginia Phelan, who taught me that, in writing, less is more. To Fern J. Hill I owe a debt of gratitude for her meticulous editing and specific suggestions, which contributed mightily to whatever merit the prose in this work displays. I owe a special thank you to my publisher, Dr. John Mabry of the Apocryphile Press. He saw possibilities in my efforts when few others did.

I also would like to thank Dr. Nancy E. Topolewski, an inspiring angel at a moment of crisis, and Mrs. Kathy Juliano of the Drew University Inter-library Loan Office for her invaluable assistance in obtaining key periodical documents for my research. Thank you to the staff of the Marion E. Wade Center, Wheaton College, Wheaton, Illinois. They led me through the legal maze of accessing Charles Williams' collection of personal notes.

I wish to express my appreciation to Selwyn Levine, M.D. and Elizabeth Varas, M.D. You know how much you helped. In doing so you became more than medical practitioners. You became friends.

Finally, thanks are in order to the William B. Eerdmans Publishing Company and Tom DeVries for allowing me to quote from their publications *Essays Presented to Charles Williams, All Hallows Eve, War In Heaven and Taliessin through Logres, The Region of the Summer Stars and Arthurian Torso*. My gratitude is extended to Will Underwood of the Kent State University Press for permission to quote passages from Roma A. King, Jr.'s masterful work, *The Pattern in the Web: The Mythical Poetry of Charles Williams*. Quotes from Charles Williams' works *He Came Down From Heaven, The Image of the City and Other Essays* and *Notes on Taliessin Through Logres: Answers to Questions from C. S. Lewis* are printed by permission of the estate of Charles Williams and the Watkins/Loomis Agency. Permission to quote from *The Collected Letters of C. S. Lewis, 1931-1949* is granted by the C. S. Lewis Company Ltd.

Works Cited

Andriote, John-Manuel. "An Introduction to Charles Williams' Incarnationalism and the Taliessin Poetry." *VII: An Anglo-American Literary Review* (1985): 73-78. Print.
Auden, W. H. "Charles Williams: A Review Article." *Christian Century* (Jan-June, 1956): 552-554. Print.
Barber, Richard. *The Holy Grail: Imagination and Belief.* Cambridge: Harvard UP (2005). Print.
Bosky, Bernadette Lynn. *British Fantasy and Science-Fiction Writers, 1918-1960* (2002). Web. 4 February 2010. <http://go.galegroup.com/ezproxy.drew.edu/ps/ retrieve>.
Boyd, Jon. *War in Heaven by Charles Williams*. 2004. Web. 10 August 2010. <http://jonboyd.org/review>.
Bulgakov, Fr. Sergius. *The Holy Grail and the Eucharist.* Trans. and ed. by Boris Jakim. Hudson, NY: Lindisfarne Books, 1997. Print.
Cavaliero, Glen. *Charles Williams: Poet of Theology*. Eugene, OR: Wipf and Stock Publishers, 1983. Print.
Curtis, Jan. "Byzantium and the Matter of Britain; the Narrative Framework of Charles Williams' Later Arthurian Prose." *Quondam et Futurus; Newsletter for Arthurian Studies 2.1.* (Spring 1992): 28-54. Print
Dodds, David Llewellyn, ed. Introduction. *Arthurian Poets: Charles Williams.* Woodbridge, UK: Boydell, 1991. Print.
Dobson, Roger and Mark Valentine, eds. *The Lost Club Journal.* 2001. Web. 2 April 2010. <http://freepages.pavilion.net/tartarus/navigatelost.html>.

Dugan, Mary H. "Uniting Christianity and Civilization: the Literary Art of Charles Williams." *Epiphany 5.1* (Fall/1984): 86-95. Web. 2 March 2011. <http://web.ebscohost.com.ezproxy.drew.edu/ehost/delivery>.

Eliot, T. S. "The Significance of Charles Williams." *The Listener.* (December 19, 1946): 894-895. Print.

Goller, Karl Heinz. "From Logres to Carbonek: The Arthuriad of Charles Williams." *Arthurian Literature I.* Ed. Richard Barber. Cambridge, UK: D. S. Brewer (1981): 121-173. Print.

Hadfield, Alice Mary. *Charles Williams: An Exploration of His Life and Work.* New York: Oxford UP, 1983. Print.

Hefling, Charles, ed. *Charles Williams: Essential Writings in Spirituality and Theology.* Cambridge, MA: Cowley Publications, 1993. Print.

Holy Bible. Gideon's 1987 ed. Nashville: National Publishing, 1978. Print.

Hooper, Walter, ed. *The Collected Letters of C. S. Lewis, 1931-1949.* San Francisco: Harper, 2004. Print.

Howard, Thomas. *The Novels of Charles Williams.* Eugene, OR: Wipf and Stock, 2004. Print.

Jacobs, Alan. *Narnia: The Life and Imagination of C. S. Lewis.* San Francisco: Harper, 2005. Print.

King, Jr., Roma A., *The Pattern in the Web: The Mythical Poetry of Charles Williams.* Kent, OH: Kent State UP, 1990. Print.

Lewis, C. S., ed. Preface. *Essays Presented to Charles Williams.* Grands Rapids, MI: Eerdmans, 1966. Print.

Malory, Sir Thomas. *Le Morte D'Arthur.* New York: Modern Library, 1999. Print.

Mackey, James. Preface. In Oliver Davies, ed., *Celtic Spirituality.* Mahwah, NJ: Paulist Press, 1999. Print.

McClatchey, Joe. "Charles Williams and the Arthurian Tradition." *VII: An Anglo-American Literary Review* (1994): 51-62. Print.

—. "The Diagrammatised Glory of Charles Williams' Taliessin through Logres." *VII: An Anglo-American Literary Review.* (1981): 100-125. Print.

McGowan, Kathleen. *The Book of Love.* New York: Touchstone, 2009. Print.

Mihal, Jay A. *The Arthurian Poems of Charles Williams: A Critical Annotated Edition.* Annapolis, MD: United States Naval Academy, 1996. Print.

Moorman, Charles. *Arthurian Triptych: Mythic Materials in Charles Williams, C. S. Lewis, and T. S. Eliot*. Berkeley, CA: U of California P, 1960. Print.

Pickin, V. M. *The Vulgate Cycle*. 2005. Web. 7 February 2009. <http://hereticemperor.co.uk/VulgRewrt>.

"Relevant." *Oxford English Dictionary*. 2010. Web. 8 April 2010. <http://dictionary oed.com.ezproxy.drew.edu>.

Ridler, Anne, ed. *The Taliessin Poems of Charles Williams*. Berkeley, CA: Apocryphile Press, 2010. Print.

Schakel, Peter. *Annotations and Study Guide to Letters to Malcolm*. Web. 19 October 2011. <http://hope.edu/academic/english/schakel/Let2malc.htm>.

Seper, Charles. *The George MacDonald Informational Web*. 2007. Web. 2 April 2010. <http://georgemacdonald.info/williams.html>.

"Significant." *Oxford English Dictionary*. 2010. Web. 8 April 2010. <http://dictionary oed.com.ezproxy.drew.edu>.

Spaeth, Paul J., ed. *Charles Williams (1886-1945) Taliessin Terms*. 2006. Web. 16 November 2007. <http://sbu.edu/friedsam/inklings/Taliessin>.

Stubbs, John Heath. "The Poetic Achievement of Charles Williams." *Poetry London, 3.11*. London: Poetry Society (1947): 42-45. Print.

Taylor, Beverly and Elisabeth Brewer. *The Return of King Arthur: British and American Literature since 1900*. Cambridge, MA: Brewer, 1983. Print.

Tennyson, Lord Alfred, *Idylls of the King*. London: Penguin, 1983. Print.

Topolewski, Nancy E. "Under the Mercy: Pastoral Dimensions of the Doctrine of Co-inherence As Set Forth in the Theology of Charles Williams (1886-1945)." *A Paper Presented to a Convocation at Drew University in Honor of the Retirement of Dean James H. Pain*. 4 May 2011. Print.

Underhill, Evelyn. *Mysticism: A Study in the Nature and Development of Man's Spiritual Consciousness*. New York: E. P. Dutton, 1941. Print.

Waite, Arthur Edward. *The Hidden Church of the Holy Grail: Its Legends and Symbolism*. Amsterdam: Fredonia Books, 2002. Print.

Wendling, Susan. "Charles Williams and the Quest for the Holy Grail." *Inklings Forever*, 7 (2010). 20 December 2010 <http://www.taylor.edu/cslewis>.

Williams, Charles. *All Hallows Eve*. Grand Rapids, MI: Eerdmans, 1981. Print.

—. Answers to Questions from C. S. Lewis. *Notes on Taliessin through Logres*. Original in Marion E. Wade Center, Wheaton, IL: Wheaton College, n.d. Print.

—. "The Cross: From a symposium, What the Cross Means to me, 1943." *The Image of the City and other Essays*. Selected by Anne Ridler with a Critical Introduction. Berkeley, CA: Apocryphile Press, (2007): 131-139. Print.

—. *The Descent of the Dove*. Vancouver, BC: Regent College Publishing, 2002. Print.

—. *The Figure of Beatrice: A Study in Dante*. Berkeley, CA: Apocryphile Press, 2005. Print.

—. *He Came Down from Heaven*. Berkeley, CA: Apocryphile Press, 2005. Print.

—. "Malory and the Grail Legend: From the Dublin Review, April, 1944." *The Image of the City and other Essays*. Selected by Anne Ridler with a Critical Introduction. Berkeley, CA: Apocryphile Press, (2007): 186-194. Print.

—. "Notes on the Arthurian Myth." *The Image of the City and other Essays*. Selected by Anne Ridler with a Critical Introduction. Berkeley, CA: Apocryphile Press, (2007): 175-179. Print.

—. *War In Heaven*. Grand Rapids, MI: Eerdmans, 1981. Print.

Williams, Charles, and C. S. Lewis. *Taliessin through Logres, The Region of the Summer Stars* and *Arthurian Torso*. Grand Rapids, MI: Eerdmans, 1974. Print

Works Consulted

Carpenter, Humphrey. *The Inklings: C. S. Lewis, J.R.R. Tolkien, Charles Williams, and Their Friends*. Boston: Houghton Mifflin, 1979. Print.
The Charles Williams Society. *Notes on the Taliessin Poems of Charles Williams*. Oxford, UK: Parchment, 1991. Print.
Dunning, Stephen. "Charles Williams and Owen Barfield: Common (and Uncommon) Ground." *VII: An Anglo-American Literary Review*. (2004): 11-30. Print.
Glyer, Diana Pavlac. *The Company They Keep: C. S. Lewis and J. R. R. Tolkien as Writers in Community*. Kent, OH: Kent State UP, 2007. Print.
Hadfield, Alice Mary. "Charles Williams and His Arthurian Poetry." *VII: An Anglo-American Literary Review* (1980): 62-70. Print.
Hillegas, Mark R., ed. *Shadows of Imagination: The Fantasies of C. S. Lewis, J.R.R. Tolkien and Charles Williams*. Carbondale, IL: Southern Illinois UP, 1969. Print.
Hooper, Walter, ed. *The Collected Letters of C. S. Lewis 1950-1963*. San Francisco: Harper, 2007. Print.
Horne, Brian. "Review Article: Poetry and Transformation." *VII: An Anglo-American Literary Review* (2008): 87-91. Print.
Jung, Emma and Marie-Louise von Franz. *The Grail Legend*. Princeton: Princeton UP, 1998. Print.
Kollmann, Judith. "Charles Williams' Taliessin through Logres and The Region of the Summer Stars." *King Arthur Through the Ages, 2*. Eds. Valerie M. Lagorio and Mildred Leake Day. New York: Garland Publishing, (1990): 180-206. Print.

Mahan, David C. *An Unexpected Light: Theology and Witness in the Poetry of Charles Williams, Michael O'Siashail, and Geoffrey Hill*. Eugene, OR: Pickwick Publications, 2009. Print.

Mahoney, Dhira B. *The Grail: A Casebook*. New York: Garland Publishing, 2000. Print.

Marino, John B. *The Grail Legend in Modern Literature*. Cambridge, UK: D. S. Brewer, 2004. Print.

Schneider, Angelika. "Co-inherent Rhetoric in Taliessin through Logres." *The Rhetoric of Vision: Essays on Charles Williams*. Eds. Charles A. Huttar and Peter Schakel. Lewisburg, PA: Bucknell UP (1996): 179-191. Print.

Shideler, Mary Mc Dermott. *The Theology of Romantic Love: A Study in the Writings of Charles Williams*. Eugene, OR: Wipf and Stock, 2005. Print.

Simmons, Joseph Hugh. "Charles Williams as Medieval Troubadour." *VII: An Anglo-American Literary Review* (2004): 83-100. Print.

Tait, Jennifer Woodruff, "Learning to Speak 'The Tongue of the Holy Ghost': An Introduction to the Poetry of Charles Williams." *Inklings Forever*, 7 (2010). Web. 2 March 2011. <http://www.taylor.edu/cslewis>.

Weston, Jessie L., *From Ritual to Romance*. New York: Anchor Books, 1957. Print.

Williams, Charles. *The English Poetic Mind*. Eugene, OR: Wipf & Stock, 2007. Print.

—. "The Making of Taliessin" *Poetry Review*. London: Poetry Society (1941): 77-81. Print.

—. "Malory and the Grail Legend." *The Dublin Review, 214*. London: Talbot Publishing, (1944): 144-153. Print.

—. *Outlines of Romantic Theology*. Berkeley, CA: Apocryphile Press, 2005. Print.

—. *Poetry at Present*. Oxford, UK: Clarendon Press, 1931. Print.

www.ingramcontent.com/pod-product-compliance
Lightning Source LLC
LaVergne TN
LVHW041338080426
835512LV00006B/517